Active for Life

Active for Life

developmentally appropriate movement programs for young children

Stephen W. Sanders

An NAEYC Comprehensive Membership Benefit

National Association for the Education of Young Children, Washington, D.C.,
in cooperation with Human Kinetics Publishers, Champaign, Illinois

Credits:

Boxes focused on skills (sequences in locomotor skills, 10; catching, 18; jumping, 26; galloping, 33; throwing, 39; balancing, 40; and rolling, 48) are adapted, by permission of the publisher, from S. Sanders, *Designing Preschool Movement Programs* (Champaign, IL: Human Kinetics, 1992).

Illustrations by Natalie Cavanagh.

Thanks to Human Kinetics Publishers for their support and cooperation.

Photographs:

© Southwestern College Child Development
 Center, Chula Vista, California, front cover
© Jean-Claude Lejeune, 2, 4, 59, 64, 86
© TTU Photography, 16, 30, 74
© Michaelyn Straub, 42
William K. Geiger Photography, back cover

**National Association for the Education of
 Young Children**
1509 16th Street, NW
Washington, DC 20036-1426
202-232-8777 or 800-424-2460
www.naeyc.org

Through its publications program the National Association for the Education of Young Children (NAEYC) provides a forum for discussion of major issues and ideas in the early childhood field, with the hope of provoking thought and promoting professional growth. The views expressed or implied are not necessarily those of the Association. NAEYC thanks the author, who donated much time and effort to develop this book as a contribution to the profession.

Library of Congress Control Number
 2002109766
ISBN 1-928896-04-9
NAEYC Product #126

Publications editor: Carol Copple
Editorial assistance: Natalie Cavanagh
Design and production: Malini Dominey

Printed in the United States of America

*To my sons Trevor and Tyler, ages 8 and 6, and all children and adults
in their quest to be physically active and healthy for a lifetime.*

About the Author

Stephen W. Sanders, Ed.D., is professor and chair of the Department of Health and Physical Education at Tennessee Technological University in Cookeville.

Steve founded the Children's Movement Center in Marietta, Georgia, where he developed one of the first preschool curricula in physical education. The center focuses on movement education of children ages 6 months to 6 years. He also served on the National Association for Sport and Physical Education committees that created the developmentally appropriate documents aimed at both school-age and young children ages 3 through 5.

He is the author of *Designing Preschool Movement Programs* (Human Kinetics) and of numerous papers and research articles defining and describing developmentally appropriate practice in movement programs for young children. Online, Steve is managing editor of the preschool physical education section of PE Central, a Website that debuted in 1996 to provide a place for physical educators to connect with one another and help them deliver developmentally appropriate programs for children.

In many early childhood programs, teachers are torn between what they know about how young children learn and preparing children for "academic" learning. But the truth is, not only does movement stimulate learning physiologically, but it also helps young children to experience concepts so they can process them cognitively.

Teachers must offer children opportunities to solve movement problems, invent their own solutions to challenges, and make abstract concepts (like high *and* low*) concrete by physically experiencing them. This is the key to learning for the young child. . . .*

Children were meant to move! Not only does movement help ensure physical fitness, but it also significantly contributes to self-esteem, prosocial character traits, creative- and critical-thinking skills, and an enhanced capacity for learning and problem solving.

By accepting the unity of mind and body, we come one step closer to genuine developmental appropriateness. After all, if we are to truly educate the whole child, we must first recognize children as thinking, feeling, moving human beings.

—Rae Pica, "Beyond Physical Development:
Why Young Children Need to Move," *Young Children*

Contents

Foreword

Early childhood educators have long understood that physical development is important, and every day preschool teachers see children happily in motion. Yet there is growing knowledge about physical development, based on research evidence, which is not widely known in the early childhood field. From this work and the leadership of the Council on Physical Education for Children in developing developmentally appropriate practice standards based on the research, we all stand to gain, through increased understanding of the learning experiences that contribute to children's long-term health and well-being.

The early childhood field, for its part, has something to contribute to physical educators: broad, in-depth knowledge of all areas of young children's development. Recognizing how much our two fields have to offer one another, we have been delighted to work with Steve Sanders, a physical educator with great interest and expertise in the preschool years. The result is *Active for Life: Developmentally Appropriate Movement Programs for Young Children*, which we believe will benefit both early childhood and physical education teachers and programs and centers for young children everywhere.

In this volume Steve emphasizes that active play, though important, does not by itself ensure that children acquire key physical skills. Developing such physical skills, research clearly shows, gives children the confidence and competence to continue being physically active and proficient throughout childhood and adult life. A child (or adult, for that matter) who feels inadequate in a certain domain generally avoids it. So the challenge is to promote early learning in ways that mesh with young children's cognitive, social-emotional, and physical development. Only when we manage to do this can we strengthen children's sense of what they *can* do—rather than reminding them of what they can't do—and inspire them to do more.

—*Carol Copple*
NAEYC Publications Editor
May 2002

Preface

Daily developmentally appropriate movement experiences have the potential to shape the lives of children in becoming physically active and healthy for a lifetime. This is an important goal.

In 1996 the U.S. Department of Health and Human Services published *Physical Activity and Health: A Report of the Surgeon General.* This was the first report addressing physical activity and health and emphasized that "Americans could substantially improve their health and quality of life by including moderate amounts of physical activity in their daily lives" (DHHS 1996). The report identifies substantial health benefits of regular participation in physical activity, including reducing the risks of dying prematurely from heart disease and of developing diabetes, high blood pressure, or colon cancer. When physical inactivity is combined with poor diet, the impact on health is devastating, accounting for an estimated 300,000 deaths per year; tobacco use is the only behavior that kills more people (DHHS 1996).

The importance of movement education for children

There are many reasons for children to be physically active. For one, physical inactivity has contributed to the unprecedented epidemic of childhood obesity currently plaguing the United States. The percentage of children considered overweight has more than doubled in the past 30 years (DHHS 1996). The importance of early education is crucial since almost half of all young people ages 12 to 21 and more than one-third of all U.S. high school students do not participate in physical activity on a regular basis. In adolescence, obesity also is associated with poor self-esteem and linked with obesity in adulthood.

The lack of daily physical activity by children and adults poses a major health concern in this country. The Centers for Disease Control and Prevention (CDC 2000) document the realities:

• Among adults today, 25% of women and 20% of men are obese.

• Diseases associated with obesity are estimated to cost almost $100 billion per year, or approximately 8% of the national health care budget.

• Physical inactivity has contributed to the 100% increase in the prevalence of childhood obesity in the United States since 1980.

In the past, many physical activity programs emphasized intensity, because the underlying philosophy of this earlier approach was that the harder the exercising, the greater the physical benefits. Many adults recall running laps in physical education classes, while a physical education teacher's bark demanded a faster pace. This emphasis on intensity may actually have been detrimental to many participants and turned off others—children and adults—from physical activity altogether. "Today's different emphasis on less intense, more moderate amounts of physical activity, and on the flexibility to vary activities according to personal preference, will encourage both children and adults to make physical activity a regular and sustainable part of their lives" (DHHS 1996, 3).

Numerous studies (DHHS 1996; CDC 2000) confirm that regular physical activity helps children to build and maintain healthy bones, muscles, and joints, and to control weight, build lean muscle, and reduce fat; it prevents or delays the development of high blood pressure, reduces feelings of depression and anxiety, and may, through its effect on mental health, increase children's capacity for learning. Participation in physical activities promotes social well-being as well as physical and mental health. In addition, from a young child's point of view, participating in daily physical activity is simply a fun way to learn and grow.

Benefits of regular physical activity

Movement is part of everyone's everyday life and has many manifestations. The urge to achieve physical skill mastery and capitalize on the body's capacity for movement is common to all children. They delight in physical accomplishment and enjoy movement for its own sake. Children use movement to express feelings, manipulate objects, and learn about their world.

Movement experiences of all kinds interest early childhood teachers because understanding of movement acquired in one context is likely to have relevance in another. It would take volumes, however, to reflect on all the uses of movement as a means of learning about our physical selves and about the world of movement. For this reason, this book focuses on providing a framework for activating developmentally appropriate practices that help children build a foundation of basic motor skills. With a grounding in the basics, teachers and children can transfer the learning of specific motor skills and movement concepts to a variety of contexts.

What concerns do teachers have?

Comments and questions from preschool teachers about children's physical activity are common and further confirm the need for support and direction.

"Should I assess children? We play games, such as Duck Duck Goose, and we dance and jump to music, and of course the kids run around outdoors. There is plenty of physical activity in our program. Isn't this enough?"

"Is it appropriate to teach a 4-year-old how to throw a ball? How would I do it with 16 children in my class?"

"We do not have the space to have a physical education class!"

"Exactly what is appropriate for young children to learn about physical activity?"

"Should I assess children's learning in physical education the same as I do other skills?"

"We have better things to do with the short period of time we have with the children; is P. E. really that important?"

The purpose of this book is to provide answers to these questions and others, based on what is known from experience and research about movement and physical activity in the lives of young children. To help, the book presents the position of the National Association for Sport and Physical Education (NASPE) as defined and illustrated in *Appropriate Practices in Movement Programs for Young Children Ages 3–5* (COPEC 2000). Central in this statement is the premise that early movement experiences assist children in becoming efficient movers of their bodies and help them develop positive attitudes about the importance of daily physical activity.

What to teach young children

From experience and research we know that children who do not develop a foundation of basic motor skills (throwing, catching, kicking, skipping, galloping, etc.) are less likely to participate in physical activity on a daily basis. Physical education and movement programs for young children should be serious in concentrating on the development of physical skills. These skills are invaluable lifetime tools that children and adults use to successfully participate in regular physical activity and to help maintain health and fitness.

Many adults maintain fitness through skill-based activities such as dance, tennis, badminton, swimming, golf, basketball, aerobics, walking, and bicycling. If children feel competent in many motor skills, they will have a greater propensity toward participating in physical activity later as adults. Movement and sequential skill development are at the center of young children's physical growth, for "no matter what the activity one cannot take part successfully if the essential fundamental movement skills contained within that activity have not been mastered" (Gallahue 1995).

This book presents a curricular foundation, strategies for teaching, and assessment ideas, and defines and illustrates specific interrelated components of developmentally appropriate practice in providing movement experiences for 3-, 4-, and 5-year-old children. Highlighted examples of these components appear in "Key Aspects in Building Quality Physical Education for Young Children" featured in a spread of pages at two junctures in the book, following Part One and Part Two. Based on national standards and professional physical education guidelines, the integrated components of appropriate and inappropriate practice (COPEC 2000), reflect a philosophy of providing early movement experiences. This approach is grounded in the knowledge that daily physical activity is necessary to ensure children's growth toward building a mature form of essential fundamental movement skills.

Why a book on national guidelines for physical education?

Emphasis on ensuring that teaching practices are developmentally appropriate is familiar to most early childhood educators. Practitioners widely apply the National Association for the Education of Young Children (NAEYC) guidelines for developmentally appropriate practice in early childhood programs and classrooms. Initially developed in the late 1980s and revised in 1997, the NAEYC guidelines help teachers plan and develop appropriate learning experiences for children. In physical education a set of guidelines for developmentally appropriate programs was developed first in 1994, and it was revised in 2000. Use of these guidelines is growing in physical education settings across the United States.

This book now shares these principles of movement education with professionals outside the physical education field—all those who work with young children in educational settings. Many early childhood centers or schools do not have physical education specialists. The responsibility for meeting the physical activity needs of young children falls mostly to program administrator/directors and classroom teachers of these young children. This book is a resource and guide.

Part One focuses on understanding developmentally appropriate practice in relation to movement education. It describes the basic premises in the NASPE position statements on movement programs for young children 3 through 5 (COPEC 1994, 2000) as well as guidelines for physical activity for young children (NASPE 2001). Part Two explores the importance of creating movement learning environments, curriculum, and teaching approaches that are in tune with the way children learn and develop. Part Three provides thinking about assessment, evaluation, and planning. A concluding chapter looks at future goals to make movement learning a full partner in education.

Useful diagrams, charts, and resources to support movement education planning appear in the Appendixes. Throughout the book, the reader will note that terms *physical activity programs, physical education programs,* and *movement programs* are used interchangeably. For purposes here these have the same meaning. A potpourri of skill learning elements comprise boxes that appear randomly throughout the book, graphically highlighted as useful, quick summaries of teaching points and skill cues.

Where to go from here?

Developmentally appropriate practice in movement education programs for young children is what we strive for in creating quality for all our children. The intent of this book is to provide teachers with a foundation of knowledge and to offer them direction, support, and encouragement in taking on the challenge of the twenty-first century— providing daily developmentally appropriate movement experiences for preschool children, with the goal of creating a new, healthier generation of Americans.

PART ONE

Making Movement Programs Appropriate for Young Children

The early years—ages 3, 4, and 5—are a critical time for children's development of physical skills. Creating a developmentally appropriate movement program for young children requires planning and an understanding of developmental characteristics of children.

Developmentally Appropriate: Understanding the Concept

"Developmentally appropriate practices," according to NAEYC (National Association for the Education of Young Children), "result from the process of professionals making decisions on at least three important kinds of information or knowledge"—

1. what is known about child development and learning—knowledge of age-related human characteristics that permits general predictions within an age range about what activities, materials, interactions, or experiences will be safe, healthy, interesting, achievable, and also challenging to children;

2. what is known about the strengths, interests, and needs of each individual child in the group to be able to adapt for and be responsive to inevitable individual variation; and

3. knowledge of the social and cultural contexts in which children live to ensure that learning experiences are meaningful, relevant, and respectful for the participating children and their families. (1997, 9)

The concept *developmentally appropriate physical education* is not new; rather, it is receiving renewed attention and reaffirmation (Barrett, Williams, & Whitall 1992). In physical education the developmental term appears early (Halsey & Porter 1958), but its use in professional literature increased after 1992 when the Council on Physical Education for Children (COPEC) in cooperation with the National Association for Sport and Physical Education (NASPE) released a position statement on developmentally appropriate physical education practices for children (COPEC 1992). The statement focused primarily on elementary school-age children.

COPEC followed its 1992 action by creating three statements on physical education practices focused on particular age group populations: middle school, secondary school, and young children. *Developmentally Appropriate Practice in Movement Programs for Young Children Ages 3–5* (COPEC 1994) signaled a growing awareness of the need to begin physical skills development early.

Structure and guidelines by NAEYC in its publication *Developmentally Appropriate Practice in Early Childhood Programs Serving Children from Birth through Age 8* (Bredekamp 1987) established the basis for defining quality. NAEYC (1997) further refined its position statement on developmentally appropriate practice, and COPEC (2000) then updated the NASPE statement on appropriate and inappropriate movement practices for young children.

In addition to the COPEC publication on appropriate movement programs for young children ages 3 through 5, a variety of books and journal and magazine articles have been published to further define and describe developmentally appropriate practice in movement programs. The developmentally appropriate movement statement defines appropriate or best practice in such a way as to provide the guidance teachers need for developing quality movement curricula and learning environments.

Quality defined

Quality movement programs are those developmentally and instructionally suitable for the specific children being served (COPEC 2000). Developmentally appropriate practices in movement programs recognize children's changing capacities to move and promote such changes. A developmentally appropriate movement program accommodates a variety of individual characteristics in children, such as developmental status, previous movement experiences, fitness and skill levels, body size, and age.

Development, in the context of the individual, has a precise meaning. It is change across time and the process underlying this change (Clark & Whitall 1989). In the teaching and learning process, this definition refers to the ongoing changes occurring in all areas of a child's learning, including motor, social, emotional, and cognitive. When teaching practices reflect this understanding, they are said to be "developmentally appropriate" (Barrett, Williams, & Whitall 1992). The practices are based on the changing characteristics of children (e.g., size, strength, problem-solving ability, self-concept).

Recognizing best practices

Appropriate movement programs incorporate best known practices, derived from both research and experience in teaching children. Resulting programs maximize opportunities for learning and success for all children (COPEC 2000). What this means in terms of creating appropriate movement learning experiences for children is that the program must take into account children's ages and individual, instructional, and cultural needs. All elements must be present for a movement activity to be considered developmentally appropriate.

Age appropriate

What is the meaning of *age appropriate* in terms of physical development in young children? Would it be appropriate, for example, to bring a group of 4-year-old children to an open play space, give each of them a ball, and then ask each child to try bouncing the ball? Would it then be appropriate to ask children to practice dribbling the ball several times in a row while moving about the room? Finally, would it be appropriate to place the children in a five-on-five basketball game? Considering a group of 3-year-olds, is it appropriate to ask children to first practice kicking a ball and then to place them in a soccer game in which they compete with others to score a goal?

For both of these age groups, it is legitimate to provide children with appropriate equipment and ask that they explore and practice individual skills of dribbling and kicking. Developmentally, children 3 and 4 years old are ready to practice individual skills such as these (see "Generic Levels of Movement Skill Proficiency" in Chapter 5). However, it is inappropriate to place all of the children in game situations. Based on the developmental levels of children these ages, most would not be ready for competitive game experiences.

Individually appropriate

An activity or learning task considered appropriate for a particular age group may still not be appropriate for every child that age. For this reason, the concept of *individual appropriateness* is added to the definition of developmentally appropriate practice for movement programs.

All 4-year-olds may not be able to dribble a ball even though the task is considered age appropriate (see "Gross-Motor Development—Widely Held Expectations, " Appendix E). Some children who are less skilled may first need to practice holding out the ball, then dropping it and catching it, before being able to continuously bounce the ball. For an activity to be considered developmentally appropriate, teachers should select learning tasks that allow a wide range of responses, meeting the individual needs of every child in the group.

An activity requiring each child to bounce a ball five times in a row, with only a practice of that single task, would not be considered developmentally appropriate. In contrast, if the teacher uses bouncing a ball five times in a row as a goal for children and, based on individual skill levels, assists each child in improving his or her dribbling skills (reflecting change over time), then the activity is age and individually appropriate.

In this discussion of individual appropriateness, it is important also to consider the other side of the spectrum. Although not typically the norm, in any given group there may be children who far exceed the skill accomplishments of others in the class as well as children with developmental delays whose skills develop more slowly. No doubt there are 3- through 5-year-old children who can dribble a ball 100 times in a row, around cones, behind their backs, and through their legs. For an activity to be developmentally appropriate for these children, they need challenges that further their individual skill development.

In a developmentally appropriate program, children who are highly skilled need activities at their individual skill levels so they change and grow over time and continue to improve in skill. One approach to assisting these children is providing similar but different learning tasks (e.g., not just dribbling, but dribbling around cones or through a maze of pathways and at a variety of speeds). Children with special needs may need further modification to the environment and learning experiences to take advantage of learning opportunities and progress toward development of physical skills.

A movement learning environment for young children that is developmentally appropriate parallels that of a developmentally appropriate early childhood classroom. All children are working at their own developmental levels, moving from one learning center or activity or task to the next. Throughout this book, examples of developmentally appropriate learning environments for movement do not look anything like the traditional physical education classes of the past that many adults participated in as children.

Instructional appropriateness

Instructional appropriateness refers to presenting tasks and learning activities to young children in a manner that reflects an understanding of each child's developmental level (see Chapter 5 for details on strategies to facilitate learning). For example, active participation is an important developmental consideration in children's skill development.

Children's participation in physical education classes consisting primarily of traditional games (relays, Duck Duck Goose, Musical Chairs, etc.) is not an effective way of maximizing young children's physical development. From the standpoint of teaching effectiveness, it is inappropriate for teachers to have children spend a great deal of time waiting—for a chance to use a piece of equipment, in line for a turn in relay races, or to be chosen for a team or group—rather than engaging in active play.

Mostly sedentary games also fail to accomplish the goals of a movement program for young children. In a developmentally appropriate program, movement exploration, guided discovery, and creative problem solving are the predominant teaching strategies employed. Children have opportunities to make choices and actively explore their environments, while teachers serve as facilitators in preparing a stimulating environment and challenging activities.

Cultural appropriateness

Culture is a powerful influence and plays an important role in children's development and learning. It should be included in any discussion of appropriate practice. NAEYC addresses *cultural appropriateness* of practices in its revised guidelines for developmentally appropriate practice.

> Culture consists of a set of rules or expectations for the behavior of group members that are passed on from one generation to the next. Cultural experiences are not limited to the artifacts or products of culture, such as celebration of holidays, foods, or music. These products are what can be seen easily but they are not the culture itself, which is that set of underlying rules of custom or habit that yield or shape the visible products. Understanding culture requires an understanding of the rules that influence behavior, rules that give meaning to events and experiences in families and communities. (Bredekamp & Copple 1997, 41–42)

Imagine 15 children in a gymnasium. To a greater or lesser extent, each child has a different understanding of the world, behavioral characteristics based on his or her family culture, experiences, and cultural expectations. Even in a group that is culturally homogeneous, each child's family and home culture is unique, and in America's early childhood settings today few groups are homogeneous. Physical activity settings offer excellent opportunities for young children to learn to recognize differences and similarities, to work with others, and to understand that different customs or cultural habits are not barriers.

Informed Practice–
Premises and Guidelines
for a New Physical Education

In discussing physical education or movement programs for young children, eight key premises guide educators' thinking, planning, and evaluating. These premises are facts or assumptions of belief that provide the foundation on which developmentally appropriate movement programs are based. The premises outlined here give teachers an overview of the physical education profession's beliefs about children and movement education and led to the creation of a developmentally appropriate movement philosophy.

1. Physically active children have greater chances of being healthy for a lifetime. The ultimate purpose of any movement program is to guide children in becoming physically active and healthy for a lifetime. Because tomorrow's physical activities may look quite different from those of today, programs need to assist young children in developing competency in basic movement skills transferable to a variety of activities—those popular today and those yet to be invented.

When basic movement skills are developed at an early age and refined during childhood and early adolescence, children are later able to go in different directions and participate in a wide variety of physical activities. Early specialization in specific sports or a limited range of opportunities to master basic skills in physical activity and movement classes limits later participation options.

For young children to grow into adults who reap the many benefits of regular physical activity, education must focus on developing basic movement skills. Programs emphasizing traditional game playing (e.g., relays, Red Rover, and others, including large-group games) do not provide for the developmental needs of young children. Mastery of basic skills (see Chapter 4 on curriculum) at an early age encourages children's development and refinement of more complex skills leading to safe and enjoyable participation in physical activity.

The National Association for Sport and Physical Education (NASPE) defines the outcome of a developmentally and instructionally appropriate program of physical education as a physically educated person.

The research is clear. Children will not develop active, healthy habits without our help. So as we teach children how to use their minds, we must teach them how to use their bodies.

—Lynn Staley and Penelope A. Portman, "Red Rover, Red Rover, It's Time to Move Over!" *Young Children*

Benchmarks of a physically educated person are

- Has learned skills necessary to perform a variety of physical activities.
- Is physically fit.
- Does participate regularly in physical activity.
- Knows the implications of and benefits from involvement in physical activities.
- Values physical activity and its contributions to a healthful lifestyle. (NASPE 1995, v)

For developmental reasons, some aspects are emphasized in early childhood, other parts as children become older. For example, preschool physical education emphasizes learning skills and regular participation in appropriate physical activity. Fitness, knowledge, and values receive more attention as children move through adolescence.

2. Movement programs and youth sports are different. Youth sports have become an American cultural phenomenon, with tens of thousands of participants as young as age 3 in competitive youth soccer, ice hockey, T-ball, and gymnastics. Such sports programs should only be provided to older children who have refined the physical skills necessary to compete with others of similar interests and abilities and are developmentally ready to specialize in one or more sports and to engage in the competition involved. Most children do not acquire this developmental readiness until the age of 6 or 7, and quite a few are not ready until much later.

In contrast, developmentally appropriate movement programs for young children are designed for *every* child—from the physically gifted to the physically challenged. The intent of these programs is to provide children of all abilities and interests with a foundation of movement experiences.

Physical activity for preschool children should emphasize self-improvement, participation, and cooperation instead of competition and winning or losing. Youth sports programs are inappropriate for 3- through 5-year-old children.

3. Children are not miniature adults. Physical activity and sports that are appropriate for adults are not appropriate for children even when adapted. Simply watering down adult sport or activity programs for children is inadequate.

Children are not miniature adults. Their abilities, needs, and interests differ from those of adults. Children learn from and need programs and activities designed specifically with awareness to their needs and differences.

Games, rules, and equipment intended for adults all too often are used in physical activities for children. For example, 3-, 4-, and 5-year-old children are often handed adult-size wooden bats and regulation-size baseballs and expected to learn how to swing a bat and hit a ball. This expectation is no more appropriate than giving a child a regulation-size basketball to toss into a 10-foot-high goal. Unfortunately, learning organized around adult activities of baseball, soccer, hockey, basketball, track, and softball fill traditional movement curricula.

Dozens of physical activity equipment catalogs advertise inappropriate sizes of equipment for young children. Unknowing center directors, for example, could find in many catalogs, and purchase, step aerobic boxes for kindergarten and preschool children that even include music for the aerobic activities. However, expecting eighteen 4-year-olds to use the proper footwork, to the same music, all at the same time—as is popular in some adult movement programs—is not appropriate. Asking children to participate in inappropriate physical activities decreases the possibilities that they will develop physical skills and increases the possibilities of frustration and turn-off to participating in any physical activity. Sometimes the activity is even unsafe for young children or harmful to their growing bodies.

4. Three- through five-year-olds differ from older children. As the understanding that children are not miniature adults is important, so is recognizing and accepting that young children are markedly developmentally different from their elementary school-age counterparts. Young children 3, 4, and 5 years old need a variety of experiences leading to more mature fundamental movement patterns. They need to practice skills of running, galloping, balancing, jumping, throwing, and catching. Development of each of these skills is a lengthy process occurring over time. Skill does not happen in a day, a week, or even months. At these ages each child needs his or her own equipment (e.g., a ball to play with) and many practice opportunities.

Those adults working with young children need to fully understand the continuum of development from infancy through the preschool years as it differs from that continuum for elementary school-age children. During the elementary years children are ready to create more mature patterns of various fundamental motor skills developed in preschool and then begin to combine these skills with others (see Chapter 6 on assessment for motor skills, benchmarks for preschool children).

5. Young children learn through interaction with their environments. This well-established premise about learning through the environment is stated in many ways: children learn by doing; children learn through active involvement with people and objects. Key in the design of developmentally appropriate movement programs for young children is that all children be active participants, not passive listeners or observers.

This premise on how children learn also relates broadly to a developmental characteristic of young children: learning is moving. To learn how to climb, throw a ball, jump, or do any other physical skill, children need a variety of practice opportunities over time and within many different contexts. For example, on their own or with introduction by a teacher, peer, or other adult, young children can learn to hold their arms out to the side while walking forward to balance on a beam. But to develop that skill, they will need many balancing opportunities, such as walking on beams, logs in woods, or lines on the sidewalk, to fully explore and develop the movement pattern in balancing. For developing all fundamental movement patterns, children must have opportunities to build basic skills in a variety of different environments.

6. Young children learn and develop in an integrated fashion. All development—physical, emotional, social, and cognitive—is interrelated. Young children's learning is not compartmentalized. Thus movement learning

> Movement . . . the necessities are your bodies, your imagination, and a willingness to try. . . . In our class we've moved like leaves blowing in the wind, bats flying, magnets attracting metal, caterpillars wrapping themselves in cocoons, and train engines pulling many cars.
> —Laurie Rodger, "Adding Movement throughout the Day," *Young Children*

experiences encompass and interface with all areas of development. Although regularly scheduled movement experiences focus on the development of physical skills, these experiences fit into the child's total development.

Movement experiences are a primary source for learning by young children. For example, as children participate in locomotor activities of walking, galloping, and skipping, they also have opportunities to express their emotions, participate socially with others, and think about and gain an understanding of how movement takes them in a variety of different directions and pathways in space.

7. Teachers of young children are guides or facilitators. Young children learn by doing. It also follows that teachers of young children facilitate children's active involvement in learning. Teachers observe and assess the needs, interests, and abilities of young children, then construct the environment with specific objectives in mind. Ultimately they assume the role of facilitators, guiding the children toward these goals. In carefully observing the children's responses and interests, teachers can adapt the learning experiences to best meet each individual child's needs.

Children can make choices and seek creative solutions, provided time and opportunity to explore appropriate responses. Engaging children in activity and extending their learning become teachers' modes of active involvement. As a result, teaching is child focused rather than subject centered.

8. Planned movement experiences enhance play experiences. A combination of play and planned movement experiences specifically designed to help children develop physical skills is beneficial in assisting young children in their development. Regularly scheduled indoor and outdoor play experiences giving children the opportunity to freely practice and develop skills enhance scheduled, appropriately designed and structured movement experiences.

Research and experience confirm that young children do not necessarily develop physical skills simply through play (Manross 1994, 2000). Thus creating opportunities for children to participate in planned movement experiences is critical to physical skill development. Structured physical activity experiences should aim at introducing a variety of different movement skills rather than focus on the young child achieving a high level of movement competence in any one skill. In addition, providing free-time, unstructured physical activity experiences encourages children to practice and apply previously learned skills.

Looking at the skill levels of fifth- and sixth-grade children who have not had physical education experiences or movement classes (or who participated in inappropriate experiences) dramatizes the fact that play alone does not guarantee development of movement skills (Manross 1994, 2000). Just as children need teachers to assist in facilitating learning and development of reading, science,

SEQUENCES IN LOCOMOTOR SKILL DEVELOPMENT

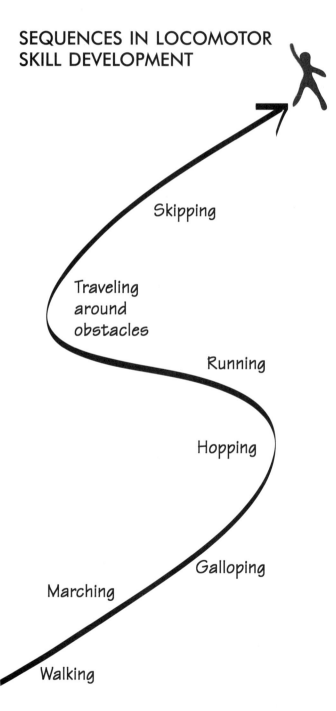

Skipping

Traveling around obstacles

Running

Hopping

Galloping

Marching

Walking

Many parents and teachers think the needs of the mind should take precedence over those of the body—as if the two can be separated! Thus these adults allocate little time to physical activity at school (and even at home).

—Rae Pica, "Beyond Physical Development: Why Young Children Need to Move," *Young Children*

and math skills, so also they need appropriate opportunities and encouragement to develop physical skills.

Physical activity guidelines

Motivated by the concerns in the Surgeon General's report (DHHS 1996), the National Association for Sport and Physical Education developed a statement of physical activity guidelines. *Active Start: Physical Activity for Children Birth to 5 Years* (NASPE 2001) outlines appropriate physical activity for infants, toddlers, and preschoolers. The guidelines suggest increasing efforts to educate young children and parents about the importance of regular physical activity, because Americans are becoming increasingly less active with each year of age and inactivity among children is now linked to future sedentary living habits as adults.

For effective promotion of lifetime activity habits early in life, developmentally appropriate physical activities should be developed in conjunction with the following NASPE (2001) activity guidelines:

1. Preschoolers should accumulate at least one hour of daily structured physical activity.

2. Preschoolers should engage in unstructured physical activity whenever possible and should not be sedentary for more than one hour at a time.

3. Preschoolers should develop competence in movement skills that are building blocks for more complex movement tasks.

4. Preschoolers should have indoor and outdoor areas that meet or exceed recommended safety standards for performing large-muscle activities.

5. Individuals responsible for the well-being of preschoolers should be aware of the importance of physical activity and facilitate the child's movement skills.

Many pieces of the physical activity puzzle are in place. The important contributions of physical activity to a healthy lifestyle are known, and guidelines exist to provide standards for creation of appropriate environment, movement curriculum, teaching approaches, and assessment practices (COPEC 2000).

What are the elements or components that make up developmentally appropriate practices for young children? How can educators go about the process of designing physical activity programs in early childhood settings? Insights that help answer these questions are included on the next pages, with ideas and suggestions on how to go about designing physical activity programs in early childhood settings.

Key Aspects in Building Quality Physical Education for Young Children

To answer the query "What works with young children?" requires first considering another question: "What approaches fit children's characteristics and the ways they learn and develop?" In the physical education and movement area, the Council on Physical Education for Children (COPEC) has responded to these questions with guidance for teachers and others who work with young children.

COPEC's guidance, which is compatible with NAEYC* guidelines for decisions about developmentally appropriate practice, is summarized below. In the left-hand column are practices widely agreed to be in keeping with young children's abilities and interests. The right-hand column describes for each area of practice a contrasting approach that is not well suited to young children's developing abilities. In some cases, the approach described on the right has a legitimate place in some kinds of programs for older children, but it is not consistent with what is known about young children's cognitive, social-emotional, and physical development.

YES = Appropriate with preschool children   **NO** = Not appropriate with preschool children

Limiting Class Size

(Y) **Teachers limit the group size in order to provide young children with developmentally appropriate individualized instruction.** No more than 9–10 children ages 4 to 5 are assigned to an adult. Younger children require smaller groups (Bredekamp 1987).

(N) Teachers organize the children in groups larger than recommended for physical activity, thereby necessitating the use of more teacher-directed methods and limiting opportunities for exploration and guided discovery.

Facilitating Maximum Participation

(Y) **Teachers use activities that do not eliminate children and frequently modify activities to enhance maximum participation.** However, they recognize that young children might need brief rest periods when participating in particularly strenuous activities. Teachers provide sufficient equipment so each child can maximally participate. The equipment includes a variety of shapes, sizes, textures, and weights to allow for experimentation and active participation, increasing the confidence and skill level of the children. Modified, nontraditional equipment is used where appropriate, such as scarves for catching and balloons for volleying.

(N) Teachers fail to maximize opportunities to learn or practice motor skills by requiring children to wait for a turn. For example, teachers encourage playing sedentary games such as "Duck, Duck, Goose" or other activities that eliminate children and provide no chance to re-enter the activity. Teachers provide insufficient equipment or only offer regulation or "adult size" equipment, which may inhibit skill development on injure or intimidate the children. Continuous, extended aerobic activity is expected.

Integrating Movement Programs and Play

(Y) **Movement programs are planned and organized by teachers as part of the total educational program.** They are included in each day's curriculum. Regularly scheduled indoor and outdoor movement experiences enhance play experiences.

(N) Teachers use outdoor and free play only as a way to get children to use up excess energy; it is characterized by a lack of goals, organization, planning, and instruction.

Allowing for Repetition and Variation

Y **Teachers provide a variety of novel learning experiences that emphasize the same motor skill,** across different environmental contexts, allowing for the gradual development of desired movement patterns. Teachers provide opportunities for the extension and refinement of these skills within instructional sessions.

N Activities are repeated without variation or are introduced and practiced only once a year, providing little opportunity for children to develop a foundation of motor skills.

Designing Learning Experiences

Y **Teachers employ both direct and indirect teaching methods.** Direct methods provide instructional models for children to replicate. Indirect teaching methods encourage children to explore and discover a range of movement possibilities. Teachers provide opportunities for children to make choices within and between tasks, while actively exploring their environment. Teachers serve as facilitators, preparing a stimulating environment with challenging activities.

N Teachers implement highly structured, teacher-directed lessons most of the time. Large group instruction is often used in which all children are expected to perform the same activities in the same manner. For example, teachers provide recorded music with verbal cues that children are expected to follow.

Facilitating Total Development

Y **Teachers design movement activities for the total development of children.** The unique role of movement programs, which allow children to learn to move while also moving to learn, is recognized and explored. Teachers provide many opportunities within a developmentally appropriate movement program for children to enhance motor, cognitive, emotional, and social development. For example, opportunities to teach such developmentally appropriate social skills as cooperating, taking turns, and sharing exist within the context of a lesson. Within the same lesson, fundamental locomotor skills are practiced while children develop spatial awareness by moving along a variety of pathways. The cognitive concepts associated with the activity and its relationship to a healthy lifestyle are reinforced. Lessons are centered on the development of the total child within a nurturing and accepting environment.

N Teachers view movement programs as separate from other areas of instruction. They are felt to be a means of "burning excess energy." For example, teachers address only the physical realm without including cognitive, emotional, and social contexts.

Guidelines continue on pages 60–61.

Source: Reprinted, by permission, from the Council on Physical Education for Children (COPEC), *Appropriate Practices in Movement Programs for Young Children Ages 3–5.* (Reston, VA: A position statement of the National Association for Sport and Physical Education/NASPE, 2000), 8–9, 11, 15, 17.

*See NAEYC Position Statement (adopted July 1996) online at www.naeyc.org/resources/position_statements/dap4.htm.

PART TWO

Designing Physical Activity Programs in Early Childhood Settings

In the developmentally appropriate preschool movement program, the responsibility of a teacher is to create an environment, situations, challenges, and activities that allow children to develop physical skills and realize their potential for movement. Physical education is one piece of the early childhood teacher's role in enhancing children's development and learning in all curriculum areas.

3

Child-Focused Environments

*The environment makes a statement about
what adults think is important for children.*
—Stephen Sanders

In the early childhood classroom learning
environment, a vibrant interaction of child,
teacher, curriculum, environment, family, and
community occurs (Taylor & Vlastos 1975).
What then should an early childhood movement environment look like?

The movement learning environment and
that of the preschool classroom are similar in
that creating an appropriate environment
requires knowledge of children and child
development principles to inform practice
(Bredekamp & Copple 1997). But then the two
environments differ—in space needs. Large-
muscle play and the development of physical
skills require space—lots of space—more than
a typical preschool classroom environment
generally has available. As a result many
teachers take movement activities out of the
classroom and into an open-space room, a gym
or multipurpose room, even a spacious hallway, or outdoors. Space is particularly important with children developing locomotor and
manipulative skills. To develop mature motor
patterns using the skills of throwing, catching,
kicking, striking, running, skipping, and so on,
children need adequate space to practice.

Appropriate movement experiences for
young children require a learning environment
that is child focused—one that uses knowledge
of the child as the key source for design and
use of space. For movement programs and
curriculum to benefit preschool children,
educators want to closely examine the ways
their learning environments take into account
space needs for children to play, practice, and
perform movement skills. This is a formidable
challenge in the many early childhood facilities
lacking large, open, safe space.

Safety is always the first concern. The
movement environment needs to be free of
obstacles (desks, chairs, sand and water tables,
easels, computers, etc.). This need should not
so intimidate teachers that they throw up their
hands and say, "Let's not have a movement
program; we don't have the space or equipment for a quality program." This chapter
provides several different approaches to
creating a safe movement environment.

Developmentally appropriate movement
learning environments respect and support
each individual child's right to learn within an
appropriate social and cultural climate. The
learning focuses not only on children's physical needs but also on their needs to be part of a
group, to work at their individual paces in
their own styles of learning, and to feel com-
fortable and confident about their abilities.

Creating the environment for movement

Components of developmentally appropriate preschool movement programs that relate directly to the learning environment include scheduled activity, class size, equipment, play, facilities, allowance for repetition and success, participation for every child, and integration of movement into other subject areas (COPEC 1994, 2000). Physical and social environments for young children should encourage and enable them to participate in safe and enjoyable physical activities (CDC 1996). Movement environments will look different based on the structure each is given by individual teachers and center administrators and depending upon available facilities.

Theoretical foundations

The developmentally appropriate movement environment parallels the child-focused classroom drawn from the work of Jean Piaget ([1936] 1963). Piaget conceptualizes that children travel through stages of cognitive development and that the force for this cognitive development comes mainly from the child.

CATCHING

Catching is a manipulative skill of receiving and controlling an object. Children progress from catching a ball, for example, with their whole body, then with their arms and hands, and eventually with their hands alone. At first they may fear the ball and pull away to protect themselves. Fears subside as children gain skill.

Cues to help young children learn to catch

• Watch the object.
• Get hands and arms in position to catch.
• Reach for the object.

Variations

Easier than catching a ball is catching a punch-ball balloon, which moves more slowly through the air. Easier still are scarves, which give children plenty of time to prepare for a catch.

Lev Vygotsky's work (1962) also influenced the development of the child-focused classroom. His developmental theory has much in common with Piaget's but puts a stronger emphasis on the social and environmental factors important in learning.

Vygotsky emphasizes that development is influenced not only by biological developmental stages but also by society. His work further suggests that environmental conditions for learning are important to the child-focused classroom. The teacher provides various kinds of assistance or support (*scaffolding*) that are geared to the child's *zone of proximal development,* which refers to the level of difficulty at which the child can accomplish a task but can do so only with the aid of an adult or more knowledgeable peer (Berk & Winsler 1995).

The child-focused movement environment, therefore, ensures a wide range of movement experiences so that children can work and learn at developmental levels that are individually appropriate. At the same time the environment is designed to provide opportunities for children to observe and learn from their teachers and knowledgeable peers. Allison and Barrett (2000) suggest that child-focused classroom environments include the following key ideas:

1. Learners create their own meaning for their educational experiences.

2. Children's learning is the focus of child-focused teaching.

3. Content is organized around big, general ideas and viewed as flexible and adaptable.

4. Content is relevant to the learners.

5. The children are seen as a community of learners.

6. Diversity enhances the potential for children's shared learning.

7. Children have important roles in assessing their own learning.

For some educators, this child-focused learning environment leads to the mistaken conclusion that the movement classroom environment is a do-as-you-like approach. This is not the case. Allison and Barrett describe the child-focused movement environment in this way:

> When [children] are given the freedom to explore and invent, outcomes are unpredictable. When teachers take the view that content is flexible, what is taught could change unexpectedly during a lesson. When diversity is valued, differing perspectives are allowed to emerge within the community of learners. . . . It does not mean that planning for learning is unnecessary…that few restrictions are imposed on the learners…that direct instruction is ineffective and, therefore, should never be used. What it does mean is that classroom environment, lesson planning, rules, and teaching methods are defined differently. . . . (2000, 12)

The physical environment

Before considering what an environment might look like complete with children and movement activities, the first step is to look specifically at the physical environment, what should be included and how the elements might be arranged. A space design that is simple and straightforward is ideal. Of utmost importance is having a large, open space free of obstacles. Next is the practical need to keep equipment in a place close to the movement space, usually a storage cabinet or closet. Teachers who have to carry equipment from another part of the building are less likely to provide movement experiences for children.

A final aspect of assessing the physical environment is determining the placement of equipment before the children arrive for movement. Locating the equipment around the perimeter of the room works best, with items of equipment near the wall's baseboard and several feet of space between each item. This arrangement provides the space children need to pick up equipment without bumping into classmates.

Teachers may find it helpful to attach shelves and hooks to the walls of the movement space or use other means for hanging equipment. Such an arrangement works well when the space is dedicated exclusively to movement activities. It is a less appropriate solution in spaces also used for lunchtime, music activities, performance of plays, and other events.

Different environments for varied needs

Not all early childhood settings are the same; so also movement environments will vary from teacher to teacher and among centers. While a number of structures may be suitable, here are three examples of appropriate environments: (1) arrangements in which children participate in similar activities at the same time (e.g., every child has a ball and is working on different ways to dribble or every child has a jump rope and is practicing rope jumping); (2) a setup in which children select activites from a variety of different stations (e.g., six to eight different stations spaced around the movement area for children's selection of practice activities); and (3) a classroom learning center (permanent space set aside in the regular classroom for a movement activity center that children can select along with those on science, sand and water, blocks, or other interests). Combinations of any of these setups also provide preschool children with well-rounded approaches to learning about movement.

1. Children participating individually in similar activities

To teach effectively within the movement setting, the teacher's aim is establishing an environment that supports learning and allows it to take place (Graham, Holt/ Hale, & Parker 2001). Visualizing what the movement environment for young children might look like is helpful. An environmental structure

> **Suggested components of preschool movement programs**
> - circle time
> - locomotor activity
> - stability activity
> - manipulative activity
> - rhythm activity

that starts, perhaps, as teacher directed and develops into child focused is a natural beginning for many teachers.

The teacher develops appropriate activities for children that have a range of movement responses. For example, a task may be as simple as "throw the yarn ball as hard as you can at the wall." Although all the children concentrate on the same activity, a variety of individual responses to the task result, based on the skill and knowledge levels of the children. Teachers might see children throwing the yarn ball to hit the wall at high, middle, or low levels. Some children decide to stand close to the wall and others stand farther away. Other children throw overhand, underhand, or use another technique to get the ball to the wall.

At this point the teacher moves freely through the room providing encouragement to individual children, facilitating skill development on an individual basis (see Chapter 5 for more on appropriate teaching strategies to use in the movement classroom). This approach of concentration on the same activity but with variation is similar to children's participation in a musical activity in which they pretend to be different animals. All the children listen and move to the same music, but they act the parts of many kinds of animals and create different movements for each to the beat of the same music. A visit to a class of preschool children entering the movement environment for the first time illustrates this concept.

In this first movement experience, the teacher has planned a variety of different learning experiences for the children. Her intention is to repeat all the activities daily for a period of time before changing or modifying the learning experiences. To establish a class structure for preschool movement, she starts with circle time and follows with locomotor, stability, manipulative, and rhythm activities.

Structuring the movement environment in a way that gives children the opportunity to learn the routine helps them understand how to work within the environment. As children are exposed to different movement experi-

ences, they begin to develop a wide range of movement skills. Instead of one activity for an entire 30-minute class period, a variety is planned. The teacher changes activities frequently (every 5 to 7 minutes during the class), so children have choices each time they participate in movement class. Teachers can use this class structure throughout the school year, adding new and different activities as children are ready for new challenges.

2. Movement stations as environments in which children select activities

A preschool movement learning environment involving children all working independently at their own skill levels but basically

Creating Movement Challenges

In a large, carpeted room, classroom teacher Mrs. Phillips introduces her 4-year-olds to the day's movement experience. As the children enter, she asks them to pick small carpet squares from a pile and carry these to the center of the room where they sit, arranging themselves in a circle with her help. Mrs. Phillips then shows the children the two rhythm sticks she holds (a drum could also be used).

"These two sticks are my stop signal. When I strike them together, I would like you to stop, freeze your body in any shape you would like, and not move." She demonstrates by striking the sticks together and freezing.

"Can you stand up, start walking around the room, and stay as far away from your friends as you can? If you see anyone getting close to you, it is your job to move away from them." The children jump up and start moving through the room. Every 20 seconds or so Mrs. Phillips strikes the sticks together, and all children stop moving. She asks if they can move backwards, and the children are off again. Each time the sticks are hit together, the children stop for about five seconds and she gives them the next challenge, such as hopping or galloping. When the children have trouble with a challenge, Mrs. Phillips strikes the sticks together to stop them so she can demonstrate how they might handle the challenge.

After four or five minutes, Mrs. Phillips sees that the children are getting tired. She strikes the sticks together doing the same types of activities requires large space and enough appropriate equipment so every child is engaged in an activity at the same time. This environment is teacher structured at first but allows opportunities for children to explore and make some choices.

What should teachers do when they have enough equipment for every child, but the space is too small to work safely? Or, what should the environment look like when space is adequate but lacks the right amount of appropriate equipment (not enough balls for every child)? And how does the environment look when the teacher tries to provide more choices for the children and a school lacks both appropriate space and appropriate equipment? Creating activity stations within the available movement space is an answer to solving some environmental dilemmas. The activity station environment (see Appendix J) illustrates the form a movement learning setting might take when space or equipment is limited or a teacher wants to give children even more choices.

With each station having a distinct skill focus, different equipment is used. The overall total movement space needed is less because single activity participation engages children within an area designated for each activity. Teachers can structure an activity station environment in many different ways, but typically each station focuses on one or two specific skills.

Single-skill specific. Teachers create learning experiences involving a particular skill or movement concept. For example, stations might focus on walking on balance beams, throwing at targets, striking a ball hanging from above, rolling a ball to knock over bowling pins, or jumping in and out of hoops. In developing the learning experiences for each station, tasks at each are varied enough to provide challenges for all children's skill levels.

The teacher's role in this environment is moving throughout from station to station, helping children who need assistance, facilitating children's learning at stations posing skill tasks of higher difficulty, or assisting where safety may be a concern. Children enter the movement learning space and move from station to station exploring each set of activities and practicing specific skills. They may stay at one station for a longer period of time than at others depending on their interests and skill levels.

At a minimum at least one activity station is needed for every three children in the class. Thus, for a class of 15 children, creating at least five stations ensures small numbers of children at any one location at any time and helps eliminate waiting for turns. Minimizing the amount of direct adult supervision necessary is important to consider in creating the majority of activity stations. The teacher should be free to move about, occasionally needing to spend

and points to several piles of beanbags against the wall (this equipment is located in small piles around the edges of the room to help children get movement equipment without bumping into each other when they walk about).

"Would you walk over without touching any of your friends, pick up a beanbag, and then balance the beanbag on your head?" "Can you balance the beanbag on your shoulder?" "Can you balance the beanbag on your elbow?" For the next several minutes the children practice balancing beanbags as suggested by their teacher. They also have ideas of their own, and Mrs. Phillips praises their creative efforts.

When this activity ends, the children place the beanbags in a small box. Next, Mrs. Phillips asks them to pick up large balloons from along the wall. The balloons spark a lively interest among the children, and they begin to bounce and strike them. Mrs. Phillips provides time for the children to play and explore without being distracted by having to listen to instructions. Next Mrs. Phillips challenges the children to practice throwing, catching, and kicking the balloons.

At the end of the active movement, the children return to their carpet squares. They sing a song, touching parts of their bodies that they used in their movement activities and corresponding with the words of the music. The children talk briefly about what they did during that day and then put away their carpet squares.

Source: Adapted, by permission, from S. Sanders, *Designing Preschool Movement Programs* (Champaign, IL: Human Kinetics, 1992), 11–12.

When children can move in general space with some knowledge of pathways, directions, and speeds, they are ready for challenges such as navigating simple obstacles. During this activity, children develop a sense of space by focusing on locomotor skills while also watching out for classmates and obstacles.

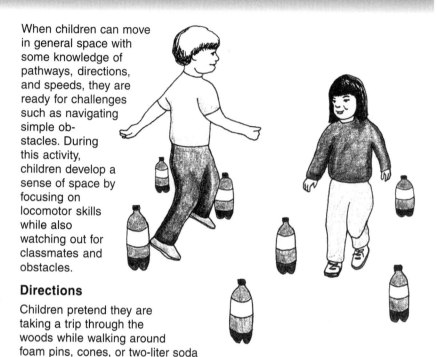

Directions

Children pretend they are taking a trip through the woods while walking around foam pins, cones, or two-liter soda bottles. Ask children to first "plant" trees by placing the obstacles themselves (teachers may need to move some trees farther apart). Different locomotor skills such as walking, skipping, and hopping can be practiced while moving through the forest.

Materials

Foam pins, traffic cones, or two-liter soda bottles. Soda bottles can be weighted with sand or gravel to keep them from easily tipping over (secure bottle caps with tape to avoid spills).

Source: Adapted, by permission, from S. Sanders, *Designing Preschool Movement Programs* (Champaign, IL: Human Kinetics, 1992), 28–29.

move nor need teacher facilitation. Teachers are free to work elsewhere with children who may need individual attention.

Children like the chance the obstacle course gives them to practice skills at their own rates and to work independently of other children. Initially, an obstacle course calls for teacher design, but as children understand the concept it is appropriate to ask them to collectively design the course or to restructure the activity at any time during the class. Obstacle courses can be structured as a station and mostly facilitate children's practice of locomotor and stability skills—tasks resembling gymnastic-type activities.

At first, in creating obstacle course sequences, placing directional arrows on the floor helps children remember which part to go to next. Some teachers develop a complete obstacle course at once, others add an activity to the course each week and develop the sequence over time. For example, one week the teacher may place hoops on the floor in a straight line so children can jump from one hoop to the next. The next week she adds boxes for children to jump off of and keeps adding new skills each week thereafter. Forward rolls, log rolls, walking on a balance beam, crawling through a tunnel, zigzagging around cones, and galloping around an obstacle are examples.

To introduce manipulative skills, teachers add to the course such activities as throwing a ball in a basket or rolling a ball down a plank.

more time at a given station. Creating a movement activity station environment is similar to creating classroom learning centers.

Multiple-skill activity. An obstacle course is a series of individual activities connected in sequence to move children from one task to the next in a predesigned order (Sanders 1992). Children practice skills, learn a sequence of movements, practice movements in sequence, begin to place individual movements together, and develop an ability to follow directions. When children participate in an obstacle course, they do not have to wait for a turn to

Active for Life

Initially young children may not be able to follow the sequence of tasks in the order intended. Many will have a favorite task. Teachers should make sure children understand the concept of moving through a sequence before adding too many challenges to the course.

If the obstacle course environment is a regular part of the movement learning experiences for children (allowing repeating the course a couple of times each week), most will gain an understanding of the concept of moving and participate easily. After a short period of time, the sequence could include as many as 12 to 15 different tasks. Designing the course so that children have a variety of sequence options makes it even more captivating and activating. Once children understand the concept of sequence, teachers will want to let them develop their own obstacle courses. Children will enjoy cooperating as they lay out the equipment and decide what skills to include.

3. Physical education classroom learning center

A learning center is an area of the regular classroom where a specific focus or learning experience is provided (Cosgrove 1992). As NAEYC suggests, "Caregivers organize the space into interest or activity areas, including areas for concentrated small-group play, being alone, art/water/sand and other messy activities, dramatic play, and construction" (Bredekamp & Copple 1997, 86). Children's work and play in a center enhances learning, reinforcing skills by getting children to use them in interesting, meaningful, relevant, and social activity.

Placing movement activity within the learning center structure ties physical activity more strongly to educational purposes. A movement center provides the opportu-

nity for children to practice individual skills that may earlier have been practiced outdoors or in the school gym. Although a classroom learning center is a good tool for reinforcing skills, it cannot compare with or substitute for a large, movement activities area and a designated time each day that provide sole concentration on the development of physical skills.

Different purposes. The reasons for having a movement learning center in the preschool classroom vary but are complementary.

First, the center serves as a place for children to practice and develop motor skills (e.g., throwing, balancing, jumping). So as children move from the classroom's construction center to language arts to dramatic play and back to the center with sand and water, they too can visit the movement learning center for motor skills practice.

A center may have a child-made target on the wall and provide yarn balls for children to throw at the target. Placing a low balance beam in the corner of the room would also let children practice balancing skills. Arranging a row of hoops on the floor gives children practice in jumping from one hoop to another.

Safety is an issue in the classroom learning center for physical activity, particularly in cramped spaces. In some preschool environments no open movement space is available to teachers, but certain skills (striking with a bat or kicking a ball) should never be part of a classroom movement learning center.

A classroom movement learning center is not better than a movement class either outdoors or in large open spaces in a gym, multipurpose room, or even a hallway. Having a movement learning center helps reinforce physical skills, and teachers must consider and mitigate the distractions movement activity might cause and its impact on other activities in the

> **Primary skills and knowledge in obstacle course environments**
> —All locomotor skills (running, galloping, skipping, hopping, etc.)
> —Movement concepts (especially Space: directions, pathways, levels; and Relationships: over, under, around, through)
> —Tasks (jumping, rolling, crawling, balancing on beams)

room. Planning types of activities that do not increase noise or visually distract other children are best.

Second, a movement learning center helps reinforce children's understanding of movement and movement concepts and integrates movement with other content areas. Movement concepts, the knowledge component of the movement curriculum, are used to modify or enrich the range and effectiveness of skill employment (Graham, Holt/Hale & Parker 2001). These concepts fit into three categories—space awareness, effort, and relationships (see Chapter 4, "Effective Movement Curriculum" for further discussion).

The preschool movement learning center that promotes an understanding of movement concepts includes experiences that help children understand pathways of movement, directions, levels, and force. These experiences complement many science and math concepts and can be integrated into a movement/science learning center. At this center children might draw pictures of different pathways or roll out lengths of playdough to form pathways.

Finally, the movement learning center can promote the development of fine-motor skills. Fine motor refers to a child's ability to use eye-hand coordination to pick up and manipulate objects (Gabbard 2000). Children's development of fine-motor skills typically occurs in the early years up to age 8. Examples include being able to visually track an oncoming ball in order to strike it with a bat, attempting to gather an oncoming ball being rolled to the child, juggling scarves, and bouncing a ball (see also Chapter 4 on curriculum).

Developmentally appropriate components of the learning environment

Details of the components of developmentally appropriate practice related to the learning environment—class size, scheduled activity, equipment, play, repetition and success, and active involvement of every child—further define the developmentally appropriate movement learning environment (COPEC 1994, 2000). Following is a discussion of several components with examples (see Chapter 4 for attention to play, repetition, and success).

Class size

In creating the preschool movement environment, class size is an important factor. The size of the class must permit a responsiveness to the needs of the children and be based on the availability of equipment and space. The number of children per class determines the approaches a teacher can use to foster successful educational experiences (Graham, Holt/Hale, & Parker 2001).

Traditional school-based physical education classes often place large groups of children together for physical activity. Although administrators give many reasons for this structuring, none of the explanations consider the developmental levels of the children sometimes placed together. As a result, three or four classes of children create a mammoth group, sometimes more than 100 children participating in one physical activity class at the same time. It is hard to justify this practice, based on any developmental guidelines educators have for children. A teacher simply cannot facilitate an enormously large number of children at one time nor be responsive to the needs of children. Such a practice places children in an unsafe and potentially harmful environment.

Large classes are accidents waiting to happen. Children need space to move. The more children in a space, the more opportunity there is for them to encounter each other, accidentally collide, or get hit with a ball or some other object, creating an undesirable social environment ("Teacher, Johnny ran into me") and the possibility for injury.

A preschool teacher in a multipurpose room or on the playground supervising 40 children—many educators possibly cannot imagine such practices exist. But they do. Developmentally appropriate practice in movement programs for young children clearly sets parameters of no more than 20 children ages 4 and 5 participating in movement experiences at the same time. Depending upon the space available and the type of activity, sometimes even 20 children are too many. Younger ages in children require smaller groups.

A basic rule of thumb, during participation in movement activities, is for the class size not to exceed the group size within the classroom. Twelve children in a preschool classroom remain together as the same 12 children going to movement experiences. It is inappropriate to send two groups of 12, totaling 24, to movement class at the same time. Young children are not used to working in a social environment so large. This class size standard, established by the National Association for Sport and Physical Education (COPEC 1994, 2000), is consistent with developmentally appropriate standards established by NAEYC:

> The group size and ratio of teachers to children is limited to enable individualized and age-appropriate programming. Three-year-olds are in groups of no more than 16 children with 2 adults, and 4-year-olds are in groups of no more than 20 children with 2 adults. (Bredekamp & Copple 1997, 135)

Scheduled activity

Chapter 1 of this book establishes the need for daily physical activity and the fact that school-based physical activity programs can play important roles in providing appropriate physical activity for preschool children. Physical activity for preschool children must be a regular part of the daily schedule. What should this component look like in practice?

Every early childhood facility has a different schedule, different physical plant and equip-

---

Movement concepts

• **Space awareness** relates to *where* in space the body moves. All movement takes place in space. Concepts include self/shared space and levels, directions, and pathways into space.

• **Effort** refers to *how* the body moves in space, involving concepts of time, force, and flow.

• **Relationship** focuses on body awareness and *what* connections the mover has with himself or herself and the environment while engaging in movement. Concepts include the relationships movement creates with one's self, other movers, and objects.

---

ment, children with different cultural needs, and a calendar of daily events that would seem to create planning conflicts. Hence it is difficult to discuss and provide examples of what a typical preschool program daily schedule might look like. Still, physical activity belongs in the daily schedule.

At least 30 minutes daily is recommended for a preschool movement class. Teachers can program movement time just as they do center time, music, lunch, or naptime. Scheduling is what it takes to make movement a daily part of each preschool child's learning experiences.

Equipment

Learning to move is like learning to read, write, or understand principles of math and science in that each requires a manipulative of some type to best develop skills and knowledge in a content area. Reading requires books and a variety of print materials to give children practice in making sounds that form words. Learning to make and record numbers, letters, and words requires the use of pencils, crayons, and a variety of other marking mediums. Understanding math and science requires resources such as weights, shapes, and assorted sizes of a variety of different items for children to manipulate.

Developing skill in physical activity requires the manipulation of balls, beanbags, paddles, scarves, hoops, ropes, and other objects. Children cannot learn to write without a pencil; they cannot learn to throw without a ball. A variety of learning materials appropriate for learning physical skills are essential in any movement program for young children to facilitate maximum participation, allow for experimentation, and increase the confidence and skill level of children (COPEC 2000).

Appropriate amount. Sufficient equipment needs to be available so every child in the class can participate without waiting. If 12 children are in the class and the teacher is working on throwing, then 12 appropriate things to throw (balls, beanbags, etc.) are essential. Each child does not need to have the exact same piece of equipment. Different types of throwing equipment (e.g., yarn balls, rubber or plastic balls, beanbags) are appropriate (see Appendix D). Teachers also want to encourage children to select and use a variety of equipment.

When equipment is scarce, the question arises, "What do I do if there is not enough equipment for each child?" One reason many teachers give for not providing a movement program for children is the lack of equipment.

The example of an activity station environment, discussed earlier, provides one strategy for dealing with limited equipment. In developmentally appropriate movement environments and curricula, not all children are doing the same thing at the same time. In fact, it is appropriate for teachers to provide a variety of activities for children each day. Ideally one

would wish that every preschool program had all the appropriate equipment needed in all areas. In reality, many preschool facilities need learning materials or could use additional resources.

One way to solve the equipment problem is to create different activity stations in the movement environment. Children rotate in small groups from one station to another, completing a different activity requiring different equipment at each station.

If a teacher has 15 rubber playground balls so that everyone in the class has his or her own, then planning is just a matter of providing a variety of tasks related to developing skills of throwing, bouncing, and kicking a ball. Many teachers, however, may have only three balls, four jump ropes, one low balance beam, six beanbags, and four hoops.

Lack of equipment is no reason not to provide movement activities for children. The teacher with some of this and that can create activity stations, one in each corner and one in the middle of the movement space. The children move from station to station practicing skills of jumping rope, throwing beanbags at a target, walking across a balance beam, jumping from one hoop to the next, and bouncing a ball. In an obstacle-course type environment children practice each skill much less than they might had they their own equipment. Obstacle-course activities should be repeated often so children have the needed skill practice.

Appropriate scale. For physical skill development, equipment for young children must be child-size—suitable for the developmental level of the children. For preschool children, learning to throw and catch using a regulation-size and -weight baseball is inappropriate. This baseball is both too small and too hard to provide young children successful skill practice. A larger, rubber ball or even a beach ball would be more appropriate.

It is also inappropriate for young children to learn how to kick a ball using a regulation-size soccer ball. A smaller, softer ball is more appropriate. For a preschool child to practice

JUMPING

Jumping is a stability skill in which the body propels itself off the ground into a brief period of flight before landing. As the first activity when introducing jumping to young children, emphasizing jumping off two feet and landing on two feet will build success and self-confidence. Activities can lead up to patterned jumping and one foot takeoffs and landings. Remember to present cues one at a time, reminding individual children when a cue is needed.

Cues

• At takeoff, bend knees and crouch when ready to jump. Swing arms forward and upward to take off from the ground.

• In flight, extend arms into the air as feet leave the floor.

• On landing, land with feet apart and body over feet.

Active for Life

striking skills using a regulation wooden bat is inappropriate as well. The bat is both too heavy and potentially dangerous to be used with this age group. An oversized plastic bat is more appropriate.

Using age-appropriate equipment enhances children's manipulative skills (throwing, kicking, volleying, dribbling, striking). In one example of catching, Payne and Koslow (1981) learned in their research of kindergartners that children's play with a large size ball resulted in significantly better catching performance than it did with smaller balls thrown from a distance of four feet. By modifying equipment, teachers can make tasks easier or more difficult. For young children, using equipment of appropriate size and weight facilitates their learning in many cases. The use of lightweight equipment simplifies the learning of manipulative skills, particularly for those children with limited strength or developmental delays.

Movement equipment is effective in helping children develop physical skills, whether materials are purchased or made by teachers or parents. Recyclable materials are a source for making scores of appropriate equipment items. Plastic soda bottles turn into bottle bats. A drain plunger transforms into a tall tee for batting. Plastic six-pack rings for holding sodas make a catcher's net. (See examples, construction, and directions in Appendix G.)

Appropriate space for storage of needed program equipment is a piece of the thoughtful planning for movement learning. Equipment must be stored in such a way so that teachers can give children access to these learning tools. As with classroom materials, children take responsibility to get equipment out and put it away. It is helpful to place individual equipment items (beanbags, balls, scarves, musical instruments, etc.) in colorful boxes, each labeled with the name and a picture of the type of item. Hanging larger items (hoops, paddles) on walls is one space solution. The teacher gets the items down, and after the activity children hand them back to the teacher to rehang.

Active involvement of every child

Every child benefits from an equal opportunity environment where he or she can readily participate and be actively involved in movement learning experiences. An activity that excludes or limits a child's participation is developmentally inappropriate and should not be part of any movement program or early childhood curriculum. Elimination activities, such as Duck Duck Goose, create an undesirable social climate as the game leaves an entire class of children sitting and inactive, while one child chases around in a circle.

Jumping: Crossing the stream

This activity helps children build their perceptual skills and muscle strength and increase their jumping ability.

Directions

Children like to jump over water, and pretending is often just as much fun as the real thing. Use string to create one or more sets of two lines that start out touching and angle away from each other. Teachers can mark the place where each child can jump across, starting on two feet and landing on two feet. Children will also enjoy finding the widest place they can jump across, and can experiment with different forms of jumping by leaping, hopping on one foot, and jumping backwards.

Materials

String makes a good marker outdoors on grass or other surfaces safe for landing. Masking tape works indoors on carpet.

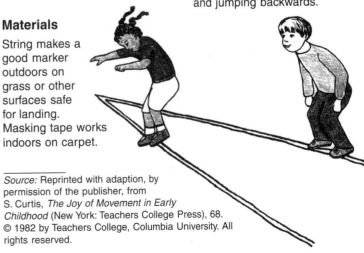

Child-Focused Environments

Making Inclusion Work in the Physical Education Setting

Environmental support—

is altering the physical, social, and temporal environment to promote a child's participation, engagement, and learning.

• Create a safe environment in which young children can move and explore. Eliminate hazards from the room such as glass mirrors, floor lamps, uncovered electrical outlets, doors and drawers that can pinch, open stairways, furniture that can topple, heavy toys, sharp edges, and breakable items.

• Be consistent when getting out and putting away equipment (i.e., balls, beanbags, and other equipment are stored in individual containers and marked with a picture or symbol).

• Lower targets and reduce distances for children who have less strength to get the object to the target.

• Use bright colors to aid children with visual impairments.

• When needed, decrease the amount of activity time and increase rest time.

• Provide surfaces that increase friction such as a carpeted floor instead of the slick surface of a wood or tile floor.

• As a safety precaution teach children with balance problems how to fall.

• Where appropriate provide a bar on the wall to assist children with stability or allow children with balance problems to stand and hold onto the wall when they need to do so.

• Use peers or adults as helpers when needed.

• Children prone to injury should wear eye and/or head protection.

Materials modification—

is modifying materials so that the child can participate as independently as possible.

• For children with impairments in strength use equipment that is of a smaller size and weight, use striking implements that have a smaller grip. Balls that are too heavy can be replaced with balloons or beach balls.

• Suspend balls from the ceiling or use deflated balls (or paper balls made of crumpled paper wrapped with masking tape) for children who have limited mobility to reduce retrieval time.

• Increase the width of balance beams or use a tape line on the floor as a modified beam.

• For catching and striking activities, use larger, lighter, softer balls but gradually introduce smaller balls to bring out a more skillful pattern.

Simplifying the activity—

is reducing the complexity of a task by breaking it into smaller parts or fewer steps.

• When throwing at a target, decrease the distance between the child and the target or increase the size of the target.

• Instead of asking a child to bounce a ball several times, ask that he or she drop and catch the ball.

• Ask children to kick a stationary ball before attempting to kick a moving ball.

• When striking with a plastic bat, increase the striking surface by using a large fat bat instead of the smaller thinner bat.

• Select all activities based on the developmental levels of children and Generic Levels of Movement Skill Proficiency (see p. 49) as opposed to chronological age or other factors.

• Allow children to participate in activities while sitting or on their hands or knees.

• When walking on balance beams, allow children to scoot or crawl across the beam (located on the floor, perhaps), with assistance if needed, or to place one foot on the floor and one on the beam. Children with visual impairments can scoot or crawl across a beam.

Activities like relay races promote feelings of inferiority in some children and create an environment that makes them uncomfortable. Graham suggests that

> Inevitably the poorly skilled, overweight children are the ones [who] end up at the back of the relay lines. They are the ones still lumbering along when the race has already been decided and, invariably, the last thing that happens in a game is remembered as the most important part. Thus the child who comes in last becomes the target of ridicule and is often blamed for the loss—even though the other team members were also slow. This may present a lasting, harmful feeling about physical activity, clearly resulting in painful and unpleasant memories of physical education or movement class. How can it possibly result in feelings of eagerness and enthusiasm toward participation in physical activity? (1992, 142)

Physical activity has a powerful influence on how children feel about themselves (Graham 1992). Even young children understand that the first rule of play is that everyone gets to play. It is important that teachers do everything possible not to turn children off to physical activity or promote negative feelings of self-worth. Teachers can have a positive influence on children's feelings and attitudes toward physical activity by planning learning experiences that do not eliminate children from participation. The type of activities children experience in the learning environment influences how they interact socially with each other not only in movement class but long after they return to their classroom and as they play and interact at home with friends, peers, and family.

Adapting for special needs

Early childhood educators know that it is important to provide all young children with an environment, equipment or materials, and experiences that assist them in learning and that meet their individual needs. The environment and learning experiences for children with special needs may need further modification to enable children to take advantage of the learning opportunities and to progress toward development of physical skills. Such modifications are vital if children with and without disabilities are to enjoy moving and to develop positive attitudes toward physical activity. Various experts (Gould & Sullivan 1999; Head Start Bureau in press) have suggested ways of making the physical education setting workable for all children (see also "Making Inclusion Work in the Physical Education Setting" opposite).

Adaptations for children with special needs are also critical for safety reasons. For example, children with less coordination may be more prone to injury (Block 2000), especially during activities that involve being off the floor (a raised beam) or in activities involving moving objects (such as throwing or striking balls). Accompanying verbal directions with signing also supports the needs of special children (see basic signing, Appendix I).

Conclusion

This chapter has provided some details on how to organize a developmentally appropriate learning environment in a preschool physical education setting. Appropriate learning environments may not look the same in every preschool setting, but all environments should be based on developmentally appropriate components and guidelines (COPEC 1994, 2000). The next chapters in this section go further, relating guidelines specific to curriculum design and teaching approaches within the developmentally appropriate preschool movement learning environment.

4

Effective Movement Curriculum

Where there is life, there is movement; where there are children, there is almost perpetual movement. Children normally run, jump, throw, catch, kick, strike, and perform a multitude of basic skills. They learn these first as general skills and later in modified versions as specific sport skills. They combine the skills into patterns of increasingly greater specificity and complexity.

—Ralph Wickstrom,
Fundamental Motor Patterns

Children and adults who are physically active on a regular basis are healthier than those who are not active. The research findings substantiating this message are clear-cut. From numerous studies it is evident that many children and adults do not regularly take part in the types of physical activities that contribute to a healthy lifestyle (CDC 2000).

The reasons for this lack of physical activity in the United States are many. But children's lack of exposure at an early age to physical skill development activities is heavily linked to limited physical activity in adulthood. Children and adults who do not possess the physi-cal skills to throw a ball, to balance while riding a bike or snow skiing, or to strike a ball with a racket simply do not integrate into their lives regular activities involving these skills.

Movement programs and play

Play supports the development of the whole child—physically, cognitively, socially, and emotionally (Rogers & Sawyers 1988). Movement programs enhance play, and play provides children with the opportunity to practice movement skills in a variety of contexts. Play alone, however, is not a substitute for helping children develop physical skills. The facts are that over time many children do not develop needed physical skills by simply playing games. Manross (1994) found that fifth- and sixth-graders who participated daily in structured skill development activities were more highly skilled than those who participated in daily physical education classes focusing on playing games.

Some structuring of physical activity is necessary to help children maximize their movement experiences. Organized movement experiences providing skill development need to be part of an early childhood program *along with* recess and other play and game experiences. None is a substitute for the other. Recess cannot fill the place of daily, organized movement experiences. Planned and organized movement classes provide children with opportunities to acquire physical skills—skills that may not be developed during play.

When and how can children learn?

The foundation for changing the way physical education and physical activity is introduced to young children is now available in a set of developmentally appropriate guidelines (COPEC 2000). In the past, a typical preschool physical education class would have the same curricular objectives and activities for every child. The class may have begun with exercises (arm raises, toe touches, push-ups, sit-ups, running laps) to stretch muscles and generally get children warmed up for large-group games and activities such as Musical Chairs, dodgeball, Red Rover, kickball, Duck Duck Goose, or relay races.

Times change. Today teachers know there are no physiological reasons for young children to stretch their muscles before physical activity. The use of stretching in sport and physical education, especially for younger children, has been based more on myth than on scientific evidence (Knudson 1998). Playing group games and participating in activities that eliminate or embarrass young children now are known as not helpful and in fact, along with those traditional stretching activities, may actually contribute to turning children off to regular physical activity.

The guidelines for developmentally appropriate practice make it clear that these activities do not provide all young children with the curricular opportunities they need to develop physical skills. Children not possessing high levels of skill were often left out and turned off to physical activity because they spent most of their physical education class time neither participating nor learning.

Children with fewer skills have always been the first ones to get hit during a game of dodgeball and thus eliminated from the game. These were the children always asked to stand in left field during kickball or T-ball games because they couldn't catch the ball. The less skilled were the ones picked last to be on teams because their classmates figured they would not help the team win the game.

Activities that are considered more developmentally appropriate for children are replacing the traditional sport and game activities that many adults remember as part of the physical education curriculum. Developmentally appropriate curriculum suggests a scope and sequence based on appropriate goals and objectives. It includes as well a balance of skills and concepts

Skills for young children to develop

Locomotor *(developed first)*

walking
running
hopping
skipping
galloping
sliding
leaping
climbing
crawling
chasing/fleeing

Stability *(developed next)*

turning
twisting
bending
stopping
rolling
balancing
transferring weight
jumping/landing
stretching movements*
curling
swinging
swaying
dodging

Manipulative *(developed later)*

throwing
catching/collecting
kicking
punting
dribbling
volleying
striking with racket
striking with long-handled instrument

(Note: Skills are examples and not meant to be all inclusive.)
*Not warm-up exercises

Source: Adapted, by permission of McGraw-Hill, from G. Graham, S. Holt/Hale, and M. Parker, *Children Moving: A Reflective Approach to Teaching Physical Education* (Mountain View: CA: Mayfield, 2001), 27.

designed to enhance the cognitive, psychomotor, affective, and physical development of every child.

Defining the developmentally appropriate movement curriculum

Curriculum is an organized framework that delineates the content children are to learn, the processes through which children achieve the identified curricular goals, what teachers do to help children achieve these goals, and the context in which teaching and learning occur (NAEYC & NAECS/SDE 1991). This chapter discusses developmentally appropriate components (COPEC 2000) related to curriculum and provides information about the content of a developmentally appropriate physical education curriculum for young children that teachers can use to make informed decisions. In addition, other developmentally appropriate preschool curriculum publications (see Appendix C) aid teachers in daily planning. Examples and suggestions for planning teaching approaches follow in Chapter 5.

A developmentally appropriate curriculum looks very different from traditional physical education curricula. The curriculum context for preschool emphasizes movement with large muscles (Wessel & Holland 1992) as opposed to playing traditional large-group games. Preschool children are still developing a range of basic motor patterns and movement skills that are furthered by movement experiences in a variety of play settings. Also, development of skills alone may be meaningless to a child unless knowledge about those skills, referred to as movement concepts, is developed.

Repetition and frequency

Traditional physical education programs typically provide curricula based on instructional units. A unit is presented to children one time each year for a period of several weeks, then another unit follows. For example, ball throwing is taught for a period of three weeks, catching for the next three weeks.

Educators now know that a curriculum such as this is not the most effective way to help children develop motor skills. If this same practice were applied to other areas of the early childhood curriculum, a class would discuss the letter *A* for two weeks, learn about colors for three weeks, set up a sand table for one week, and possibly never go back to these activities during the remainder of the school year. The practice makes no sense based on what is known about how young children learn.

Developmentally appropriate practice suggests that children be provided with a variety of learning experiences throughout the year emphasizing all areas of motor skill development. This practice ensures that children get needed skill practice over time. A clear difference between the effective and less effective movement education teacher is evident in the amount of time children spend on physical skills (Siedentop 1991; Rink 1996).

The value of practice over time may seem obvious, yet continuous repetition of skill development experiences is frequently neglected (Graham, Holt/Hale, & Parker 2001).

GALLOPING

Galloping (locomotor skill) is an exaggerated slide step composed of a step and a leap. The front leg is lifted and bent, then thrust forward to support the weight. The rear foot quickly closes to replace the supporting leg as the front leg springs forward again. Children begin moving forward by stepping on the front foot and bringing the rear foot forward. Galloping is an easy movement pattern. Many children learn how by age 2 or 3.

Cues
• Take a big step forward.
• Keep one foot in front of the body at all times.

Variations
Children can be challenged to gallop forward and backward, in different pathways, and at different speeds.

Performance of tasks, especially those that require a higher degree of skill is significantly influenced by practice and repetition (Gabbard 2000). The more children practice, the better skilled they become.

Skill building progression

The movement curriculum should be so designed that later learning experiences build on earlier learning experiences. Children develop fundamental movement skills and abilities first before being introduced to more complex or difficult skills (Motor Development Task Force 1996). Developing fundamental movement skills is part of what is referred to as motor development. Motor development encompasses the abilities essential to physical movement and the subsequent acquisition of motor skills.

Educators view this development as an extensive, more or less continuous, lifelong process beginning at birth and continuing through adult life (Wickstrom 1977; Gabbard 2000; Gallahue & Osmun 2001). Preschool children need sufficient practice opportunities in order to achieve a foundation of basic skills.

These basic skills and knowledge make up the foundation of movement in a developmentally appropriate preschool movement program (see "Movement Concepts 'I Am Learning,'" Appendix A, for one way to look at the movement framework). In inclusive classrooms, adaptations may be necessary not just to the environment but of materials and activities.

Attention to children with special needs

Many early childhood classes include children whose development requires adaptations to physical activities or equipment. When children are in wheelchairs or orthopedic braces, adaptations of gross-motor equipment are often necessary. For other kinds of special needs, simpler adaptations may suffice. For instance, the teacher may place a balance beam on the ground, at least initially, rather than elevate it.

Children with developmental delays often have low muscle tone and strength. Finding movement more difficult, they move less—and this leads to further weakness. Extra planning and encouragement are needed to engage these children in physical activities. The same can be true of children who are physically fearful or intimidated by their highly active peers.

Skill themes as the foundation

Fundamental movement skills are those movements and combinations of movements that a child is neurologically ready to develop and refine during the preschool years (Poest et al. 1990). Movement skills may be subdivided into categories sometimes referred to as skill themes (Graham, Holt/Hale, & Parker 2001). The actual physical movements or skills educators want children to learn and perform comprise the skill themes. Several different skill theme frameworks have evolved, but for purposes of discussion here three categories are used: locomotor skills, stability skills, and manipulative skills (see "Skills for Young Children to Develop" on p. 32).

Locomotor skills are those in which the body is transported in a horizontal or vertical direction from one point in space to another (Gallahue 1995). Fundamental locomotor skills include walking, running, hopping, skipping, galloping, sliding, leaping, climbing, crawling, chasing/fleeing.

Stability skills are movements in which the body remains in place but moves around its horizontal or vertical axis. These skills also include dynamic balance movements in which a premium is placed on gaining or maintaining balance in relationship to the force of gravity (Gallahue 1995). Turning, twisting, bending, stopping, rolling, balancing, transferring weight, jumping and landing, stretching, curling, swinging, and swaying are all skills involving stability.

Manipulative skills are vigorous and involve giving force to objects or receiving force from objects (Gallahue 1995). The movements include throwing, catching and collecting, kicking, punting, dribbling, volleying, striking with rackets, and striking with long-handled instruments. Manipulative skills are most frequently associated with playing games.

Movement concepts

Movement concepts are the knowledge component of the movement learning curriculum. Learning the concepts helps to modify or enrich the range of skills and the effectiveness of children's use of skills (Graham, Holt/Hale, & Parker 2001). Educators place these concepts in three categories: space awareness, effort, and relationships (see "Concepts of Movement—The Knowledge Component" on the next page).

Skill themes relate to what children can do with their bodies; a concept such as space awareness relates to where the body moves in space. All movement takes place in space. Space awareness movement concepts include space location, directions, levels, and pathways. Effort movement concepts refer to how the body moves in space. These concepts include the components of time, force, and flow. Relationship movement concepts refer to the ways the individual, while moving, projects himself or herself and relates with other people and the environment. These concepts encompass body awareness and

movement relationships/roles with other movers and objects. Graham, Holt/Hale, and Parker suggest that

> The distinction between movement concepts and skill themes can be clarified by a comparison to grammar. Skill themes are always verbs—they are movements that can be performed. Movement concepts are always modifiers—they describe how a skill is to be performed. This distinction also clarifies how movement concepts are employed to embellish, enhance, or expand the quality of a movement. A verb by itself—strike, travel, roll—is typically less interesting than one that is modified by an adverb—strike hard, travel jerkily, roll smoothly. Skills can stand by themselves. You can roll or gallop or jump, but you can't slow or high or under. Concepts modify skills. (2001, 25)

Body awareness: Mirrors and shadows

These related games increase children's awareness of body movements and shape through experimentation with moving physical images. *Mirrors* provides children with nonlocomotor movement practice and helps broaden movement vocabularies by exposing children to someone else's actions. *Shadows* encourages skill growth in balance and flexibility in addition to promoting body awareness in a similar manner to *Mirrors*.

Directions

In *Mirrors*, children pair off and stand facing each other. While standing in place, partners trade off performing and imitating a series of simple movements. Variations include having one child stand in back of the performer and another in front or having one child lead a group. In *Shadows*, individual children or groups move various body parts to observe the shadow shapes they make. Children make big, small, wide, narrow shadows; use only their arms or legs to create designs; and work together or individually to create animal or monster shapes.

Materials

No special materials are needed other than a bright light for indoor shadow play.

Source: Reprinted with adaptation, by permission of the publishers, from R. Pica, "Beyond Physical Development: Why Young Children Need to Move," *Young Children* 52/6 (1997): 7; and S. Curtis, *The Joy of Movement in Early Childhood* (New York: Teachers College Press), 54, 58. © 1982 by Teachers College, Columbia University. All rights reserved.

Concepts of Movement—The Knowledge Component		
Space awareness (where the body moves)	**Effort** (how the body moves)	**Relationships**
location self-space and shared-space **directions** up/down forward/backward right/left, sideways clockwise/counterclockwise **levels** low/middle/high **pathways** straight/curved/zigzag	**time** fast/slow **force** strong/light **flow** bound/free	**of body parts** round, curved, straight, narrow, wide, twisted, big/small, like/unlike **with other movers and objects** near to/far from, over/under, in front/behind, on/off, together/apart, facing/side-by-side, around/through **in roles with people** leading, following, mirroring; in unison, alternately, solo, partnership, group

Source: Reprinted, by permission of McGraw-Hill, from G. Graham, S. Holt/Hale, and M. Parker, *Children Moving: A Reflective Approach to Teaching Physical Education* (Mountain View, CA: Mayfield, 2001), 26.

"I am learning" summarizes it

One framework for looking at the interrelatedness of skill themes and movement concepts is to think about the curriculum in terms of the awareness teachers want children to have about what they are learning (see Appendix A for an outline summary of themes, concepts, and learnings, in preschool movement experiences).

A child asks the question, "What am I learning?" and responds, for example, in terms of the movement curriculum, "I am learning *what* my body does or what it can do" (pinpointing skill theme or action awareness). Children can make these identifications: "I am learning *how* my body moves" (effort awareness), "I am learning *where* my body moves" (space awareness), "I am learning about the *relationships* my body creates" (body awareness).

Many of the movement concepts are not just concepts that relate to skill development and the movement environment. Concepts of *fast/slow*, *around*, *up*, *forward*, and *straight*, for example, all are found in the academic classroom learning environment. Thus movement concepts integrate easily throughout the early childhood curriculum, as they are already in many settings.

Combining themes and concepts to create learning experiences

Young children learn about movement concepts as they practice skill themes. Chapter 5 focuses on how teachers can design appropriate lesson experiences to help children understand movement concepts as they develop physical skills. Learning about concepts and developing skills go hand and hand. For example, in a developmentally appropriate movement program, a preschool child might be asked (1) to throw (manipulative skill theme) a ball at a target placed at a high level (space concept); (2) balance (stability skill theme) on a beam (relationships concept); or (3) climb (locomotor skill theme) sideways (space awareness concept) at a slow speed (effort concept) across (relationships concept) a playground structure. In a developmentally appropriate early childhood movement program, planning experiences that help young children understand movement concepts is as important as assisting them in the development of physical skills.

Themes/concepts wheels

To illustrate the interaction between skill themes and movement concepts, three movement wheels illustrate locomotor, stability, and manipulative skills (see "Locomotor" at right and larger reference images of all three wheels in Appendix B). Using these wheels, teachers can better understand the interconnectedness of the early childhood movement curriculum and thus plan appropriate experiences for young children. The depicted wheels are adaptations of the "Movement Analysis Framework Wheel" created for elementary teachers (Graham, Holt/Hale, & Parker 2001, 28).

Preschool children learn in ways that differ from those of elementary school-age children. Hence the adapted wheels create a curricular framework specific to young children's needs. The restructuring and naming of the wheels' content keeps in mind that not every teacher may have a background for directing a developmentally appropriate movement program for young children.

Each wheel consists of five concentric circles. The inner circle shows one of the three specific categories of movement (locomotor, stability, manipulative) and in the adjacent circular band related specific skills. The outer rim highlights the three categories of movement concepts (effort,

space awareness, relationships), and the two circular bands inward give a breakdown of the specific concepts in these categories.

The three wheels (locomotor, stability, manipulative) are helpful tools for teachers in planning appropriate movement activities for preschool children. A wheel's inner, shaded section (skill theme and encircling related skills) is stationary. The outer section (comprised of concepts and related knowledge components) rotates. By pinpointing any specific skill within a skill theme and rotating the outer section to align any movement concept, an unending variety of explorations is possible.

To envision an exploration, the teacher moves the wheel's outer section so that Pathways (one concept of where the body moves and in what way: straight, curved, zigzag) aligns with a Locomotor skill, such as Galloping. This result suggests that children develop this movement skill by Galloping in *curved*, *zigzag*, or *straight Pathways*.

To integrate more than one movement concept at a time, rotate the wheel to align the same skill with an additional concept. For instance, a child Walking (skill) in a *forward Direction,* on a *curved Pathway, fast* in *Time,* and *leading* a classmate *With herself* integrates several concepts. Not all the concepts shown on the wheel relate directly to every skill. For example, a teacher would not ask children to engage in Leaping *under* or Throwing *counterclockwise.*

What's important in a developmentally appropriate movement program for young children is for the young child to develop physical skills plus an awareness of how movement concepts relate to those skills. Limiting children's movement experiences simply to throwing or kicking a ball (manipulative skills), for example, without introducing the concepts of kicking *hard,* throwing *high,* or kicking *under,* fails to provide the knowledge base young children need to become movement proficient.

Determining how much time to spend

A developmentally appropriate preschool movement program is very full in terms of content important for children's early learning. How to bring this content together in developing appropriate learning experiences is discussed next in the chapter on teaching practices. But busy, time-pressured yet conscientious teachers often ask, "How much time should children spend working with each skill and concept?" To a great extent, the amount of time depends on the developmental levels of the children and the particular setting.

In practice it is difficult to separate out which of all the concepts to be learned should be first. When a child gallops across the playground, concepts of space awareness (Where my body moves), effort (How my body moves), and relationships (My body creates) all come into play as her galloping takes different pathways, assumes varying time speeds, and creates relationships to objects and other children in the environment.

During their initial movement experiences, young children need to spend a great deal of time learning about space and participating in space awareness activities before dealing with effort and relationships. All movement takes place in space. Understanding space is a safety consideration. When children do not develop an understanding of where their bodies are in space and do not take responsibility for their movements

Throwing: Newspaper delivery

This throwing game helps children learn how to throw for accuracy and follow through, make estimations, self-evaluate, and persevere in practicing this skill. It is an excellent activity for beginning throwers of different abilities, as the choice of short throwing distances will help children develop accuracy and reinforce a sense of success. Generally, children make reasonable choices when choosing for themselves.

Directions

Children throw newspapers at a drawing of a house attached to the wall above a large box. Each child can choose the distance from which to throw and can continue throwing unless someone else is waiting.

Materials

Several newspapers folded approximately 4 inches wide and fastened with rubber bands, soft enough to absorb force when they hit the wall. Newspapers can be wrapped in plastic bags to avoid making marks on the wall or staining children's hands with ink. A large box and a large drawing of a house are also needed.

Source: Adapted, by permission, from M. Torbert and L.B. Schneider, *Follow Me Too: A Handbook of Movement Activities for Three- to Five-Year-Olds* (Menlo Park, CA: Addison Wesley, 1993), 114–15. Available from NAEYC.

Active for Life

through space, they tend to bump into classmates or trip over equipment. For young children, space is the first frontier, not "the final frontier" as Star Trekkers suggest.

It is clear which skills should be introduced first to children and which should receive the most attention. The difficult part is that all children do not learn at the same rate or in the same way, so it is problematic to say that all children should have experiences in developing one skill before another. Other considerations are necessary when children have developmental delays.

Developmentally, children learn some skills before others. In addition, some skills take longer to develop. Children learn to walk before they run. They learn striking with body parts (e.g., foot, head, hand/palm) before striking with an instrument (paddle, bat). Thus from a developmental perspective, young children should spend more time with locomotor and stability skills than with the manipulative. In developing physical skills, children move through a sequenced developmental progression (see "Progression in Children's Development of Physical Skills" on the next page). The first skills children learn are the locomotor movements; the last learned are manipulative skills. Of course there is substantial overlap in this progression. Children are still extending and refining a given set of skills when they move on to the next set in the progression. In practice, experiences in all of the skill areas should be provided. Depending on the skill levels of individual children, however, teachers will spend more time on some skills than on others.

Application of skills and concepts

Movement skills and concepts form a curricular base for preschool physical activity. Children who develop a base of fundamental movement skills and related conceptual

THROWING

Throwing (manipulative skill) is a basic movement pattern that propels an object away from the body. The thrower grasps the object with one or both hands, prepares the body and builds throwing momentum, propels the object away from the body, and follows through while maintaining body balance.

Cues
- Step forward with the foot opposite the throwing arm.
- Bring your arm up and behind you before you throw.

Variations

Children initially find it easier to throw a large ball such as a punching balloon. At first, encourage children to toss the balloon only a few feet into the air, holding both hands on either side. As their skills develop, they will learn to throw higher.

knowledge will move throughout elementary and secondary school, using these skills in a variety of different contexts. Educational gymnastics, games, dance, and fitness are the content areas in which basic learned skills and concepts are explored further and applied.

Opportunities for children to apply skills and concepts to daily life are essential and can happen in a variety of different contexts. For example, the good in knowing how to throw is fulfilled in the child's having the opportunity to play a game by throwing at a target on the wall or into a bucket, at the same time building confidence by knowing that she or he is able to apply the skill. Why have children only learn balance by walking on a balance beam when they could apply the skill during educational gymnastics if teachers added balancing and other skill learning in a gymnastic obstacle course or sequence? Young children can feel they are participating in real games and gymnastics and using their skills.

Young children need many opportunities in a variety of contexts to explore movement learning and to practice specific motor skills from the three skill theme categories. They accomplish this practice by working individually on specific skills or by using one or more skills in a dance, gymnastic, fitness, or gamelike learning experience. Preschool children are just beginning to develop competency in physical skills, and the emphasis should be on individual skill development activities in a play-based learning environment.

The approach for teachers of young children is planning movement experiences that let children develop a foundation of skills and conceptual knowledge about those skills without being concerned about applying skills in program-structured traditional physical education content areas of games, dance, gymnastics, and fitness. The COPEC (2000) statement on developmentally appropriate movement programs lists content areas as specific components (see "Key Aspects in Building Quality Physical Education for Young Children" on pp. 12–13 and 60–61).

Inclusion of traditional adult-oriented games, dance, gymnastics, or fitness activities in early childhood or preschool movement

Progression in children's development of physical skills

locomotor skills
jumping and landing (stability)
balancing (stability)
transferring weight and rolling (stability)
kicking and punting (manipulative)
throwing and catching (manipulative)
volleying and dribbling (manipulative)
striking with rackets/paddles (manipulative)
striking with long-handled instruments (manipulative)

programs has little support among educators because these activities are considered developmentally inappropriate. Most young children lack the prerequisite skills to participate in such structured activities. Considering the inclusion of activities of this type is like asking preschool children to read a book before they understand the alphabet or to do addition problems before they have a working understanding of numbers. Simply stated, group games and gymnastic, traditional dance, or fitness experiences have no place in preschool movement programs.

BALANCING

Being in balance (stability skill) means having an even distribution of weight on each side of a vertical axis, and can be either *static* (in place) or *dynamic* (while moving). The center of gravity is over the base of support. For young children, being on balance simply means not falling over. This is critical in developing physical skills. Young children should first learn about weight bearing and stillness by balancing on different body parts as both wide and narrow bases of support. Eventually children can balance on equipment.

Cues
- Use a wide base of support (static).
- Extend arms to the side (dynamic).

Variations
For children who may have difficulty balancing on equipment, a balance beam may be placed on the ground, at least initially, rather than elevated.

Conclusion

In closing this chapter, it is important to focus briefly on fine-motor development. Fine-motor skill refers to a child's ability to use eye-hand coordination to pick up and manipulate objects (Gabbard 2000). Development of fine-motor skills usually occurs during the early years (see expectations for 3- through 5-year-olds, Appendix F). Activities such as stringing beads, putting together puzzles, cutting, sorting cards, drawing, writing, and copying are typically part of an early childhood program's daily routine.

Fine-motor development progresses slowly during the preschool years, but by kindergarten children are more readily able to engage in activities demanding such skills and for longer periods of time, with less frustration. This development has importance for children's manipulative skill progress in physical education.

Although fine-motor skill development receives attention in the early childhood classroom, the lack of daily, planned gross-motor experiences remains a concern. Gross-motor skills, also referred to as basic motor skills or fundamental movement skills (skill themes previously referred to) are those basic movement patterns (walking, running, throwing, jumping, rolling, striking, etc.). They form the foundation for more advanced and specific movement activities. Developing these skills—locomotor, stability, and manipulative—calls for creating a scheduled time of at least 30 minutes each day as a part of the early childhood curriculum. Planned learning experiences help children develop an important base of gross-motor skills.

What's ahead?

A developmentally appropriate physical education curriculum designed for young children assists them in not only exploring and acquiring a foundation of physical skills but also in building a basic understanding of the concepts related to those skills. Chapter 5 furthers this exploration of the curriculum framework, offering teachers suggestions on planning appropriate learning experiences to assist children in gaining movement skills and understanding the concepts.

While expectations for children's physical growth and activity in a particular classroom should come from teacher observation, developmental characterizations of children by age group (see "Gross-Motor Development—Widely Held Expectations," Appendix E) provide rough guidelines that enable teachers to start general program planning.

5

Appropriate Teaching Practices

Movement skill learning is sometimes viewed simply as the product of some form of activity designed to improve children's motor performance, with little attention given to the processes involved. Such a view is incomplete and limited in scope.

—David L. Gallahue,
"Transforming Physical Education
Curriculum," *Reaching Potentials*

In the developmentally appropriate preschool movement program the teacher's responsibility is to create an environment, situations, challenges, and activities that allow children to develop physical skills and learn about their potential for movement. In NAEYC's revised position statement (1997), one of the guidelines for decisions about developmentally appropriate practice describes the important role of early childhood teachers in "teaching to enhance development and learning." NAEYC takes the position that

Teachers accept responsibility for actively supporting children's development and provide occasions for children to acquire important knowledge and skills. Teachers use

their knowledge of child development and learning to identify the range of activities, materials, and learning experiences that are appropriate for a group or individual child. This knowledge is used in conjunction with knowledge of the context and understanding about individual children's growth patterns, strengths, needs, interests, and experiences to design the curriculum and learning environment and guide teachers' intentions with children. (1997, 17)

A 2000 National Research Council report establishes a compelling foundation for quality teaching in preschool, suggesting that research shows a range of teaching strategies are appropriate for use with young children eager to learn:

Effective teachers also organize the classroom environment and plan ways to pursue educational goals for each child as opportunities arise in child-initiated activities and in activities planned and initiated by the teachers.

This panoply of strategies provides a tool kit from which the teacher can select the right tool for the right task at the right time. Children need opportunities to initiate activities and follow their interests, but teachers are not passive during these initiated and directed activities. Similarly, children should be actively engaged and responsive. . . . (Bowman, Donovan, & Burns 2000, 8–9)

Approaches in teaching movement to preschool children

No single theory of learning explains learning or the lack of it for all situations; therefore, there is no single approach to teaching (Rink 2001). In movement education, developmentally appropriate practice for preschool children embraces a wide range of teaching strategies. The most commonly used with young children are exploration, guided discovery, and creative problem solving.

As with most preschool learning, movement calls for an approach that is mostly child focused and engages children in learning through activity. When children engage in active learning, they typically evidence a higher level of involvement than they show when they experience only direct instruction in the classroom.

In traditional movement settings based on direct instruction, the teacher is the transmitter of all knowledge, instructing children to do particular tasks in specified ways. The teacher closely directs movement activities and learning. For example, she may ask all children to throw, kick, or strike a ball in a specific way requiring a narrow range of appropriate responses. Or the teacher may assign partners and equipment, tell children exactly where they should stand during activities, and require them to listen quietly.

By contrast, in a child-focused movement setting, the teacher often develops activities that children encounter upon entering the movement environment. The activities are not designed to lead children's learning in a particular direction but to give children choice among the activities and, in effect, encourage them to direct their own learning (Stork & Engel 1999). When there is a separate room for the movement program, children are included in decisionmaking related to how it is arranged and maintained and rules for behavior. The teacher, rather than actively directing children's learning, serves as a facilitator, a resource person, and a mentor.

Becoming a child-focused teacher in the movement environment

One difficulty in shifting from traditional instruction to a more child-focused approach is that the former has perpetuated itself for generations of teachers and learners. Many teachers teach as they were taught, by teachers using direct instructional techniques. Often too, individuals trained in teacher-controlled instructional methods find it more difficult to use child-focused approaches.

It is important to understand the difference between

Learning to navigate space: Camping in the great outdoors

This activity helps children navigate spatial relationships by interacting with materials in a dramatic play context.

Directions

Teachers and children can prepare the space by scattering cones and hula hoops or carpet squares around the space, with a large parachute or bedsheet in the middle. Cones can then become mountains or tents, while the hula hoops or carpet squares become lakes. The teacher calls out directions such as "Take a hike" (children walk about the space), "Climb a mountain" (children step over cones), and "Jump in a lake" (children—no more than two—jump into a hula hoop or onto a carpet square). The activity concludes with a "Bear scare," during which everyone stands, kneels, or sits under the parachute or bedsheet as directed.

Materials

Hula hoops or carpet squares (enough for half of the class), cones or milk jugs (one per child), and a parachute or large bedsheet.

an environment in which the teacher calls all the shots and one that is more child focused. To help teachers, Stork and Sanders (1999) compare effective and less effective approaches in the preschool movement education environment (see the chart on the next pages). The outline guides teachers through 10 steps to systematically compare responsibilities in contrasting teaching situations.

Ensuring child success—Matching activities to a child's abilities

Teachers can successfully create appropriate learning activities and experiences that motivate children to practice movement activities and develop physical skills. Research suggests that for learning/gaining a new skill, children should experience success in the practice of that skill at a rate close to 80% of the time (Brophy & Good 1986; Siedentop 1991; Graham 1992). This means that all of the movement activities created by the teacher need a range of appropriate responses to ensure that each child is successful at each activity at least 80% of the time.

As children participate in movement activities, they may experience what Csikszentmihalyi (1975) defines as *the state of flow.* The concept is simple and relates to many educational and play experiences, not only movement activity. Flow deals primarily with the motivational aspects of an activity. An activity providing optimal challenge in relation to the child's skills creates an in-the-flow environment.

When an activity or task is too difficult, the child may become frustrated and stop the practice. An activity needs to be challenging but achievable to be considered developmentally appropriate. If the task is too easy, the child may bore quickly and also stop practicing. A child in a state of flow finds the task so motivating she or he wants to continue to practice or explore. The word *task,* sometimes associated with a teacher-directed style, is also simply another way to communicate movement activities or movement experiences.

An activity or learning center that invites children to throw a beanbag at a large target on a wall by requiring every child to stand the same distance from the wall to throw is developmentally inappropriate. To make the activity appropriate, a teacher could design a setup that gives children opportunities to throw from a variety of distances, enabling them to experiment and find the position offering challenge but from which they experience success.

Some children might hit the target 8 out of 10 times standing 3 or 4 feet from the wall. Others might stand 20 feet away and be able to hit the target 80% of the time. It is not important how far away children stand. What's important is that each child have the opportunity to find out at what distance she or he will be successful—in the flow—and thus want to continue the activity and learn from the experience.

The process of skill proficiency

By understanding the levels and stages children go through in developing new skills, teachers are better able to provide developmentally appropriate activities or movement tasks. Learning a new skill is a process. Children who do not have opportunities to go through the process and experience skill development in a sequential progression may simply not develop competence in given skills.

Gallahue (1995) describes learning as "a relatively permanent change in behavior." The challenge for movement educators, as he notes, is that

> The actual learning of a new movement skill is an internal process that can be observed only indirectly through the product of one's movement. Unfortunately movement skill learning is sometimes viewed simply as the product of some form of activity designed to improve children's motor performance, with little attention given to the processes involved. (1995, 133)

Levels and stages

In learning new movement skills, children go through different levels and stages of

Comparing Approaches in the Preschool Movement Education Environment

Effective	*Less Effective*
1. Construction of physical knowledge through experimentation	
Activities are presented in the context of "Can you . . . ?"or "Show me how you . . . " and with emphasis on skill practice and investigation.	Teacher-controlled instruction is oriented toward reproduction of specific skills.
Children choose their own partners, equipment, and individual personal space.	Teachers assign partners, equipment, and spacing.
Children can change and use equipment in their own ways.	Teachers indicate a narrow range of specific behavioral responses.
2. Knowledge of developmental sequences	
A knowledge of stages theory is applied in relation to the development of physical skills.	Activities are presented in a rigid schedule related to sport seasons and designed to accomplish all objectives in the curriculum.
A process (intratask variation) allows children to choose levels of maximum achievement.	All children perform the same skill at the same level of difficulty.
Informal, continuous assessment is used to modify tasks.	Assessment occurs at the end of the unit.
	Children who are highly skilled receive more favorable treatment.
3. Systematic records of progress for each child	
Progress is determined by process variables, not the product.	Progress is determined by product measures, which are biased against children with certain characteristics.
Activities are presented that accommodate different ways of using skills in order to engage individual children's interests.	All children are expected to participate equally in activities of the teacher's choice.
4. Systematic records of planning and activity objectives	
Teachers use spiraling techniques or relate similarities in individual skill development.	Teachers use the same lesson plans each year with very little adaptation.
Teachers monitor responses and make changes to maintain children's interests.	Children's show of disinterest is interpreted as off-task behavior.
5. Encouragement of interactive learning between and among children	
Children choose and work toward common goals.	Children work on narrow, teacher-directed goals.
Children are encouraged to suggest changes for games or activities.	Play is discouraged in favor of close adherence to traditional rules and game conventions.
Children discuss and choose appropriate activity changes.	Very little accommodation of individual needs occurs within the context of teacher-directed activities.
Teachers provide opportunities for participation at different levels.	Teacher talk predominates. Children must be quiet while teachers speak.
The so-called gym is an engaging, noisy place.	

Note: *Effective* suggests practices that are appropriately child focused; *less effective* are practices that are overly teacher directed.

Effective	*Less Effective*

6. Children sustain the natural consequences of their behavior

Teachers allow children to monitor their own play.	Teachers take on the role of referee or authority on fairness.
Teachers allow children to work out their own difficulties, stepping in only when children experience an impasse.	Teachers provide immediate solutions by which all parties are bound.

7. Consideration of children's interests and experiences

Teachers introduce activities by asking about children's experiences.	Teachers introduce activities as "This is what we have to do next."
Activities are purposeful in ways that are fun.	Teachers warn that poor performance or lack of participation will result in lower grades.
Teachers look out for difficulties and derive appropriate changes in play or rules.	Teachers observe primarily for the purpose of determining who is "doing it right."
Children are asked to talk about their favorite movement equipment at home and to suggest ways to improve play activity in the classroom.	Children are not allowed to use their own equipment, and their ideas are patronized.

8. Encouragement of children's independence and responsibility

Children choose activity stations.	Class schedule is rigid; all children advance through one progression at the same pace.
Time is given for sustained practice.	Intervention occurs only for the class as a whole instead of for individuals.
Opportunities to rest from activity are built in.	Time-out is sanctioned as an objective for children's failure to exhibit responsible behavior.
Appropriate intervention allows children to work out skill deficiency through practice.	Rules and protocols come only from the teacher.
Teachers encourage ideas and contributions.	
Children follow up on their responsibilities.	
Rules and protocols are collaborative.	

9. Stimulation to consider problems and to reason logically

The curriculum shows a recognition that skills and concepts overlap specific activities and also have relevance in other academic areas.	Skills and concepts are taught in a context limited to the activity at hand, if at all.
Children use skills and concepts in a variety of contexts to improve depth of learning.	The curriculum is based on the assumption that children will develop an appreciation for skills and concepts simply through participation.
Opportunities exist for children to discover new contexts for skills and concepts.	No opportunities are given for children to explore movement beyond the activities presented by the teacher.

10. Eliciting thoughtful responses through a variety of questioning styles

Questions help children organize their ideas and make informed choices.	Questions cause children to guess at the one correct answer, known only by the teacher.
Questions help to represent the teacher as learning with the children.	The teacher uses wrong answers as an opening to pedantic instruction.
The teacher is an active listener.	The teacher fails to address deficits in children's knowledge, providing patronizing responses to incorrect answers and responding superficially to children's misconceptions.

Source: Adapted, by permission, from S. Stork and S. Sanders, "A Developmental Approach to Early Childhood Physical Activities," paper presented at the NAEYC Annual Conference, New Orleans, 1999.

development (Gallahue 1995). Graham, Holt/Hale, and Parker (2001) call these levels the Generic Levels of Skill Proficiency (GLSP). They suggest that there are observable characteristics as children move through each stage of skill development. The GLSP is divided into levels of precontrol, control, utilization, and proficiency (Stanley 1977).

Precontrol level (beginner). The lack of ability to either consciously control or intentionally replicate a movement characterizes this level when children are just getting the idea of how to perform a skill. They should have a variety of opportunities to explore and to discover how to do new movements. A child at the precontrol level might be observed throwing a ball into the air and then not knowing where it is for attempting a catch. The ball is controlling the child.

Control level (advanced beginner). This level is characterized by less haphazard movements. The body appears to respond more accurately to the child's intentions. A child at the control level might be observed throwing a ball into the air and then being able to position her body in readiness for the catch. The child may not catch it every time, but at least she knows where the ball is and is ready to attempt the catch. Children at the precontrol and control levels are in the discovery and exploration stages of physical development (Gallahue 1995). They need opportunities that permit them to experiment and find the many ways a skill might be done.

Utilization level (intermediate). Increasingly automatic movements characterize this level. A child at the intermediate level is ready to join actions of one movement skill with another and begin to place those skills into gamelike situations. A child might be observed throwing a ball high into the air and catching it 8 out of 10 times or being able to play a game of catch with a friend without spending most of the time chasing the ball.

Proficiency level (advanced). Somewhat automatic movements that begin to seem effortless characterize this level. Children at the proficiency level are challenged to participate in games and activities requiring a high level of skill and are able to participate in competitive activities.

Observable characteristics of each of the generic levels of skill proficiency are helpful in guiding teachers (see "Generic Levels of Movement Skill Proficiency"). Generic levels are not age or skill specific. Often older children and even adults are at the precontrol level for skills they were never exposed to or did not have ample time to practice. In addition, a child may be at the *precontrol* level in catching, skipping, and striking with a paddle but at the same time be at the *control* level in throwing and galloping and at the *utilization* level in kicking.

Preschool children typically have not had the movement experiences and skill practice to match up to the characteristics defined in the utilization and proficiency levels of movement skills. Certainly a 4-year-old could have the skill characteristics outlined in the utilization level, but it is not the norm.

ROLLING

Rolling (stability skill) is the act of transferring weight to adjacent body parts around a central axis.

Rolling sideways like a log is the simplest rolling activity for children to learn and the easiest to introduce. Children can also rock back and forth on their backs, which builds the motor control necessary to learn forward rolls. Teachers who are uncomfortable with forward rolls should not introduce them.

Cues to help children learn to roll:

• When rolling sideways, keep legs together.

• When rolling sideways, keep arms at the side, over the head, or bent at the elbow and held against the chest.

• For rocking, remind children to keep their backs rounded by either placing hands and feet in the air or pulling knees to the chest.

Generic Levels of Movement Skill Proficiency: Observable Characteristics

Precontrol level

— Child is unable to repeat movement in succession; one attempt doesn't look like another attempt to perform the same movement.

— Child uses extraneous movements that are unnecessary for efficiently performing the skill.

— Child seems awkward and frequently doesn't even come close to performing the skill correctly.

—Successful performances are characterized more by surprise than by expectancy.

—When the child practices with a ball, the ball seems to control the child.

Control level

—The child's movements appear less haphazard and seem to conform more to the child's intentions.

—Movements appear more consistent, and repetitions are somewhat alike.

—The child begins to perform the skill correctly more frequently.

—The child's attempt to combine one movement with another or perform the skill in relation to an unpredictable object or person is usually unsuccessful.

— Because the movement isn't automatic, the child needs to concentrate intensely on what he or she is doing.

Utilization level

—The movement becomes more automatic and can be performed successfully, with concentration.

—Even when the context of the task is varied (slightly at first), the child can still perform the movement successfully.

—The child has developed control of the skill in predictable situations and is beginning to be able to move skillfully in unpredictable situations. The child can execute the skill the same way consistently.

—The child can use the skill in combination with other skills and still perform it appropriately.

Proficiency level

—The skill has become almost automatic, and performances in a similar context appear almost identical.

—The child is able to focus on extraneous variables—an opponent, an unpredictable object, the flow of travel—and still perform the skill as intended.

—The movement often seems effortless as the child performs the skill with ease and seeming lack of attention.

—The movement can be performed successfully in a variety of planned and unplanned situations as the child appears to modify performance to meet the demands of the situation.

Source: Reprinted, by permission of McGraw-Hill, from G. Graham, S. Holt/Hale, and M. Parker. *Children Moving: A Reflective Approach to Teaching Physical Education,* 5th ed. (Mountain View, CA: Mayfield, 2001), 95.

As teachers plan skill development activities for preschool children, their focus will be appropriate skill development tasks for children with the physical characteristics described in the precontrol and control levels. This does not suggest that planning is easier. Precontrol and control experiences should provide a broad range of different activities and tasks for children.

Developmental considerations

Developmental characteristics of an age group provide rough guidelines that enable teachers to make broad program plans (Bredekamp & Copple 1997). The physical characteristics of preschool children are an important consideration in developing specific activities. To list some of the general characteristics of an age group is appropriate, but it is impossible to state, for example, that all 4-year-old children have specific characteristics. Some widely held expectations for gross-motor development (see Appendix E) serve as beginning understanding for movement education teachers in knowing the physical characteristics of preschool children. This knowledge is the foundation for planning appropriate movement learning experiences.

Development of movement learning experiences

An earlier discussion of the variety of developmentally appropriate movement environments (see Chapter 3) gives teachers ideas for learning experiences to assist children in developing physical skills and acquiring knowledge about these skills. Now the focus is on how teachers plan learning experiences.

First, understanding how to develop and present content or curriculum for preschool movement education is important. Next is developing a format for planning appropriate movement learning experiences. Planning is a process to take seriously. Many different approaches exist from which to select, based on individual teaching styles, classroom learning environments, selected curricular activities, and the individual needs and skill levels of the children. Key components of the process follow.

Plan appropriate content

To provide developmentally appropriate movement curriculum and learning for preschool children, teachers engage in a process of content development (Graham 1992; Rink 1993; Graham, Holt/Hale, & Parker 2001).

Developing content involves (1) informing learners about what they will be doing, (2) providing appropriate tasks or experiences, (3) refining the tasks as children are ready, and (4) providing challenges or application experiences to motivate children to continue to practice. This pattern is similar to the process preschool classroom teachers go through daily in planning for children's learning.

Inform learners and set the stage

Children, even preschool children, have a right to know up front the focus of the movement learning experiences. Teachers need not go into great detail, but it is appropriate to tell children what they are going to be doing, as these examples suggest:

"Now we are going to work in our water-play, sand, and science learning centers."

"It is time for movement and music, and you will explore marching to the beat."

"Today we will learn all about the letter *Q*."

"In our learning centers today, you will explore different ways to jump and land."

An activity may go in a different direction than that intended by the teacher or the curriculum, but engaging children in the plan enables them to be flexible. Openings for movement classes are similar to regular classroom morning circle times when teachers greet children and discuss the day's activities.

Teachers who effectively communicate to children the focus of an activity are setting the stage, scene, or set for what will follow by introducing children to it. The process of informing is sometimes referred to as *set induction*. Preschool-age children are at the precontrol and control stages of development. Thus this informing communication— set induction—needs to be less specific and to take place at the beginning of the class as well as several times throughout the activity. Developmentally, it is inappropriate to carry a single activity through an entire class period of 30 minutes (see Chapter 3 for examples of learning stations versus whole-group activities).

Presenting several different learning experiences during movement time helps young children begin building a foundation of different skills. For example, setting up seven or eight learning stations, all having to do with learning about throwing, can be fun and stimulating for the entire class. The teacher sets the stage, asking children to move throughout the room and try out activities at each of the stations. Her invitation might be, "Today we are learning about throwing. See if you can hit the target at each of the learning stations." Now is also a good time to involve children in discussing safety and managerial concerns about their participation.

The teacher does not specifically direct children's learning or give answers. She may begin a class by saying, "Today, in jumping, I would like you to focus on how many different ways you can land on your feet without losing your balance or falling over." To help children understand different ways to land and still remain on balance, the teacher invites them to move throughout the movement space, jumping over and off of a variety of low obstacles.

Identify tasks or movement activities

Tasks are the activities or actions teachers ask young children to do to explore movement in many forms. In the preschool movement environment, the teacher typically designs tasks or learning station activities he or she believes all children can successfully accomplish 80% of the time. The idea is to design the activity in a way that enables children to participate and to be successful. The teacher moves throughout the space, observing individual children and providing feedback on their movement performances.

Suggesting changes in a task or activity may be appropriate to make it easier or more difficult for some children but not for reasons of having the entire class of children trying the same task the same way. Changing an activity for an individual child to make it easier or harder, is referred to as *intratask variation* (varying the activity). Using this technique, a teacher modifies tasks based on the abilities and interests of children. The philosophy behind the intratask variation supports the teacher's role of facilitating learning by helping a child participate in an activity of interest and be successful.

For example, the teacher introduces a learning activity, suggesting that children get a ball and then saying, "See how many different

Spatial awareness: Weather walks

This interpretive game helps children develop awareness of space, relative distance, and relationships within space in addition to using the body as a means of expression.

Directions

Have children dramatize various weather conditions by walking as if they were feeling each kind of weather in turn. Teachers can suggest possible weather conditions such as windy, puddles after a rain, very cold, very hot, and walking in autumn leaves. The class can weave a story around the weather, becoming more involved when children can imagine the feeling of a particular weather condition. Or children can act out a daily weather report, starting with a sunrise and ending with a sunset, or can pretend that they are walking in various substances or places (e.g., on eggs, around a sleeping tiger, in a dark house).

Source: Adapted, by permission, from M. Torbert and L.B. Schneider, *Follow Me Too: A Handbook of Movement Activities for Three- to Five-Year-Olds* (Menlo Park, CA: Addison Wesley, 1993), 144–45. Available from NAEYC.

Precontrol Proficiency Level

Traveling

in general space
with different locomotor movements
in different ways
with imagery
in rope pathways

Jumping

and landing using different patterns
for distance
for height
over a swinging rope

Balancing

on different bases of support
on a wide base of support
in different body shapes
by traveling on low gymnastic equipment
by traveling and stopping in balanced
  positions
on boards

Kicking

a stationary ball from a fixed position
a ball at large targets
after approaching a stationary ball
the ball by tapping (as in soccer)

Throwing

a yarn ball against the wall
at a large target

Catching

a rolling ball
from a skilled thrower
in a drop-catch sequence
by tossing to self

Volleying

by striking balloons in the air
by striking a balloon forward
by striking with different body parts
by striking lightweight objects

Dribbling

by bouncing a ball down and catching it
by bouncing a ball down (dribbling)
continuously
and walking

Striking (with rackets and paddles)

balloons (lightweight paddle)
a suspended ball

Striking (using long-handled instruments)

a stationary ball (hockey or golf)
a puck toward large targets (hockey or golf)
a ball off a batting tee (bats)
a ball dribbled in self-space (hockey)
a ball while traveling slowly (hockey)

Precontrol is the first level of experimental activity/exploration. **Control** level represents the next progression in skill.

Source: G. Graham, S. Holt/Hale, and M. Parker, *Children Moving: A Reflective Approach to Teaching Physical Education,* 5th ed. (Mountain View, CA: Mayfield, 2001).

Children to Explore

Traveling

using different locomotor patterns (run, leap, skip, hop, gallop, slide, etc.)

with music

an obstacle course

in different pathways

at different speeds and changing speeds

Jumping

and land using basic patterns (2 feet to 1 foot, 2 feet to 2 feet)

a standing long jump

over low obstacles, hoops

rhythmically

with a self-turned rope

forming a body shape during flight

Balancing

with a counterbalance

with a stationary balance on equipment

with inverted balances

in traveling on a large apparatus

on a balance sequence

on stilts

on balance boards

Kicking

on the ground

in the air

for distance

to a distance zone

to targets

a rolling ball to a partner from a stationary position and dribbling around stationary obstacles

Throwing

overhand, underhand, or sidearm

overhand at a stationary target

underhand to hoops

a Frisbee

for distance

and catching with a partner

Catching

in different places on the body

with a scoop

the rebound in throwing against a wall

and throwing with a partner

Volleying

by striking a ball noncontinuously with different body parts

in striking a ball upward, underhand pattern

in striking a ball toward a wall, underhand pattern

to the wall, overhand pattern

to a partner, overhand pattern

by playing Keep It Up

Dribbling

all the time

at different heights with the body in different positions

in different places about the body while remaining stationary

and traveling

Striking (with rackets and paddles)

up and down

forward against the wall

on both sides of the paddle

to wall targets

a ball rebounding from a wall

continuously

Striking (using long-handled instruments)

a stationary ball on the ground (hockey or golf)

a ball into the air (golf)

for distance

suspended objects using a bat

while traveling and changing pathways (hockey)

with a bat while throwing a ball into the air

a pitched ball

ways you can find to dribble the ball with your hands." A task of exploring a variety of different methods of dribbling is open enough that most all children can achieve a level of success. Using this technique, the teacher then moves throughout the room observing the children's activity. Seeing that Jenny really needs more of a challenge, the teacher suggests combining the dribbling in a walk throughout the room. Peter is having difficulty even bouncing the ball. This time the teacher offers an idea, "Why don't you try to drop the ball and catch it?" Appropriate tasks allow children to succeed at the task approximately 80% of the time.

The chart on the previous spread of pages outlines some precontrol and control activities for selected skills. Using these broad categories, teachers can develop more specific tasks or learning activities. For example, at the precontrol level "jump for distance" is an idea for content that fits the skill of jumping. With this content focus, teachers can plan a variety of activities or learning stations that give children opportunities to develop jumping skills by jumping different distances, such as "jump across a rope on the floor," "jump as far as you can," and "jump across the hoop."

Use cues or principles to refine activities

A cue word or phrase is like a movement secret that helps a child learn or perform a skill better (Graham 1992). Cues support children in focusing on that part of the skill they are working on. The task could be "Throw a beanbag, and see if you can hit the target." Many preschool children may have difficulty initially in performing this skill.

Exploring first. Because young children progress through skill levels (precontrol and control, toward utilization and proficiency), providing specific cues at the start may be inappropriate. Young children need to explore a variety of performance options before receiving cues to refine their skills. For instance, suggesting to 3- and 4-year-olds at the precontrol skill level that they step with the opposite foot when throwing may be premature, trying to refine a skill before children are ready and thus not developmentally appropriate. Likewise, it is inappropriate for the preschool teacher to suggest to the class in the set induction, "Today we are going to work on stepping with the opposite foot."

Using cues. Some methods of performing skills are more efficient than others, and teachers can help children by offering cues such as those shown here. The cues are based on biomechanical principles for efficient movement. For example, for the young child to catch a ball, she must hold out her hands somewhere in front of her body. Holding the hands behind the body or out to the side would be different ways to attempt catching a ball but not very efficient.

In another example of cue use, it is biomechanically sound to suggest doing a forward roll by tucking the chin into the chest. Even though the roll can be done without tucking in the chin, it would not be as efficient

Cues

—for practicing locomotor skills

Walking
- swing arms
- head up
- balance stops

Running
- swing arms
- bend elbow
- head up
- balance stops

Skipping
- lift knees
- hop and land on one foot
- hop and land on the other foot

Galloping
- same foot forward

Hopping
- arms out
- knee up

Chasing
- watch hips
- corner

Fleeing
- fake changes of direction
- change speeds

Dodging
- change levels
- change directions

—for practicing stability skills

Jumping and landing
- bend knees
- swing arms
- land both feet at same time
- balance landing

Balancing
- maintain stillness
- tighten muscles
- extend arms
- keep center of gravity over base of support

and might even be dangerous, resulting in an injury to the young child's neck.

Checking child readiness. Teachers are unlikely to ask all preschool children to attempt using the same cue at the same time in performing an activity. Suggesting specific cues to individual children, in the process of facilitating learning (intratask variation) helps each child refine a skill. By watching a child explore, experiment, and struggle with the best way to hold a pencil, the teacher will discover the appropriate time in the child's development to suggest a different approach (a cue): "Holding the pencil like this makes it easier (more efficient) for you to write your name or to draw."

While it is inappropriate to have all children working on one cue at the same time, it is appropriate to say to an individual child who is developmentally ready, "Try the skill this way and see what happens." An appropriate cue is given for a skill being practiced (see locomotor, stability, and manipulative "Cues" at left; vocabulary and cues in Appendix H).

The preschool teacher moves through the movement environment spotting any children who are not having success throwing a ball to hit a target on the wall. She sees that one child is frustrated with an activity and wants to quit. The young child throws with the right hand but does not step forward on either foot. He is ready for help. Cues used in throwing could facilitate this child's learning. The teacher poses the question, "What would happen if you stepped forward when you throw the ball?" Now the child can experiment, exploring this principle of throwing to learn if it is actually a better way to throw.

Scaffolding as a process. Assisting children in their mastery of specific tasks is sometimes referred to as scaffolding. The process suggests that teachers focus children's attention on the task and keep them motivated and working throughout the practice session by dividing the task into simpler, more accessible components and directing the child's attention to the task's essential, relevant features or cues. The role of the teacher is to help children avoid unnecessary frustration and encourage their independent problem solving during practice of the task (Moll 1990).

Create skill challenges or applications

Children need large amounts of time for practice to move from the precontrol level of skill development to the control level and on. Providing children challenges is one way to increase the amount of skill practice. Creating challenges is a teaching technique for maintaining children's interest without changing the activity or task.

Challenges are tasks or activities made measurable (or more fun) by the teacher. In making a task measurable, the teacher motivates a child to try it in a different way. The task, "See if you can throw your beanbag and hit the target," becomes "Can you hit the target three times in a row?" Other examples include the task, "Show me you can bounce the ball," which leads to "How many times can you bounce the ball with one hand?" or "How many different ways can you find to bounce the ball?" A challenge such as "Can you stand on one foot?" grows to "See if you can balance on one foot while you are counting to 10!"

Making new challenges is something young children do naturally on their own and teachers do frequently in the early childhood classroom in the process of facilitating individual learning. Challenges are but another teacher strategy for providing children with success-oriented learning activities.

Planning the learnings

In creating a movement education plan, teachers focus on curricular learning experiences (see Chapter 4) they want to provide for children and the type of activities at each learning station. A format for planning preschool movement learning experiences (see "Guide for Creating a Movement Learning Plan") reflects a focus on skills of throwing, balancing, and jumping. The plan's design works for an activity station learning environment where children move on their own, one station to the next, exploring and practicing different tasks. Its format suggests that teachers list the skills, concepts, learning objectives, equipment, and protocols. In this example children will work on three skills: throwing, balancing, and jumping. The teacher exposes them to the concepts of straight pathways, forward and backward directions, hard force, and over as a relationship.

The objective in all preschool movement learning is providing children with opportunities to explore and develop physical skills. Specific curricular objectives enrich the education plan and, as in the learning plan (opposite), suggest that as children move through different activities they are exploring and learning how to throw, to balance, and to jump.

Teachers find it useful to list the equipment needed and the protocols they will follow during the class. Protocols are the rules or procedures children and teachers decide on to ensure safety and fairness to all participants. These protocols may already be familiar to children. Others may be new to them, based on the uniqueness of the movement environment.

The set induction of the plan takes a short period of time—usually not more than 30 seconds to two minutes. The teacher describes to the children what they will explore during the class and also goes over any guidelines necessary for the children. Many young children are visual learners and quickly pick up on how to do activities by observing and watching others (Sanders 1993). It's important to give just enough information to get them started, then facilitate ideas or introduce additional tasks to children as the class goes along.

Central to the plan is creating activities and experiences for children's participation. Open-ended tasks and activities give children more opportunity to be successful in whatever they choose to participate. At the end of or during the movement time, it is appropriate to bring the children together and talk briefly about what movement actions they experienced.

Teachers may invite children to tell what they learned at particular learning stations, giving them an opening such as this, "Today we tried to find out how many different ways there are to bounce a ball. Who wants to share an idea?" This short engagement period also provides a transition time for children before they move back into the classroom where moving about is perhaps more restricted.

Guide for Creating a Movement Learning Plan

Skills: throwing, balancing, jumping

Movement concepts: During throwing, children learn the concept of throwing the ball with **force**; during balance activities children focus on moving in **straight** lines both **forward** and **backward;** and during jumping activities children experience the concept of jumping **over**.

Learning objectives: Explore ways to throw at a variety of targets; practice and discover different ways to balance while moving across a line on the floor and across a small balance beam; explore ways to jump over objects and land on balance without falling.

Equipment: Yarn balls, beanbags, two-liter soda bottles, small balance beams, hoops, and jump ropes.

Protocols: Teacher takes a short period of time to remind children of the rules for movement time: (1) look before moving; (2) help classmates in getting out and putting away equipment; (3) everyone stop to listen when the teacher claps her hands two times.

Activity station descriptions:

 # 1 Throwing activity station—Yarn balls and beanbags are in a box. The station has targets (art projects made earlier in class) taped on the wall. Two-liter soda bottles are fun for children to knock over with balls or beanbags.

 # 2 Balancing activity station—Masking tape on the floor in straight and zigzag lines are for children to walk on; small balance beams (two inches off the ground) are placed so that taped lines connect to them and children get the idea of an obstacle balance course as they move from tape line to beam and back to tape line.

#3 Jumping activity station—Jump ropes are laid on the floor in a straight line for children to jump over; two ropes form a stream that children can jump over from one bank to the other. Hoops are in a straight line so that children can jump over hoops from one to the next.

Set induction: The teacher tells children that they are going to work on throwing, balancing, and jumping. Because these are new stations, the teacher spends a short period of time taking them around to the different stations and helping the children become familiar with the equipment and activities.

Activity ideas within individual stations

1.1. How many different ways can you find to knock down the bottles?
1.2. Can you hit the target on the wall?
1.3. To strike the target, is it better to throw with more **force** or less?

2.1. Practice walking in a **straight** line on the tape line.
2.2. Can you walk **backward** on the tape line?
2.3. Can you walk **forward and backward** on the balance beam?
2.4. How many different ways can you think of to move along the lines and across the beams?

3.1. Explore jumping **over** the hoops and across the rope lines. How many different ways can you find to jump and land?
3.2. Can you jump **over** the stream?
3.3. Jump **forward and backward** over the rope.

Closing: You look like you had fun in the movement period today. What is important to know about throwing? Jumping? Balancing?

Challenges

— How many bottles can you knock down with one throw?
— How many times out of five can you hit the target?

— Can you walk all the way across the balance beam without stepping off?

— See if you can land on both feet at the same time three jumps in a row.
— How many times can you jump back and forth over the rope without stopping?

(Note: Bold typeface in activity ideas indicates movement concepts.)

Conclusion

Meaningful, developmentally appropriate learning experiences take many forms. A child-focused approach to teaching is not a roll-out-the-ball approach in which children do as they please and teachers hope that learning is taking place. Exploration, interaction, and understanding are credentials of a movement curriculum that is child focused. Teachers develop opportunities for children to interact with the movement environment so they can explore big ideas. Preschool movement teachers find ways to increase the opportunities for young children to develop a foundation of basic physical skills that later can be refined and then applied to a variety of different physical activities.

Children's development of physical skills during the preschool years, facilitated by informed teachers, is fundamental and crucial to the goal of helping all children become physically active and healthy for life.

Continued from page 13.

Key Aspects in Building Quality Physical Education for Young Children

YES = Appropriate with preschool children

NO = Not appropriate with preschool children

Developing Health-Related Fitness

(Y) Teachers demonstrate positive attitudes towards fitness and recognize the importance of children valuing physical activity as a lifelong habit. Children experience the joy and learn the value of exploring their movement abilities as a lifetime pursuit. Teachers convey the concept that fitness is a byproduct of participation in appropriately designed movement programs. For example, after an appropriate period of continuous locomotor movement, children are asked to discuss what happens to their bodies during vigorous movement participation.

(N) Teachers disregard explanations of why activity is important and plan non-motivating activities where children regularly wait to participate, wait for equipment, run laps, perform calisthenics, or participate in follow-the-leader video programs.

Implementing Assessment

(Y) Teachers use authentic assessment based on the scientific knowledge of children's developmental characteristics and ongoing observations of students in activities. This information is used to individualize instruction, plan objective-oriented lessons, identify children with special needs, communicate with parents, and evaluate the program's effectiveness. Teachers encourage children to do self-assessment as it relates to improving skill performance. For example, teaching children "cue words" for fundamental movement skills will allow them to self-evaluate their performance relative to the cues.

(N) Teachers assess children solely on the basis of test scores, such as physical skills tests, norm refrenced tests, and standardized fitness tests. Teachers use tests to merely audit performance rather than improve it. Assessment indicators are not shared with the parents or the child.

Promoting Success for All Children

(Y) Teachers provide children with opportunities to practice skills at high rates of success, adjusted for their individual skill levels, and within a "try again" and "effort equals improvement" environment. When needed, teachers provide an environment in which children can practice skills independently of other children to avoid the frustration and anxiety of low skill proficiency. For example, children can practice catching a ball that rolls consistently down a chute. Teachers do not use competition between children as a motivator.

(N) Teachers direct children to perform activities that are too easy or too hard, causing boredom, frustration, and/or misbehavior.

Teachers place children in large group or partner situations in which their success is dependent on other children, resulting in a lack of skill development. For example, when children throw and catch with a partner, more time is spent chasing the ball than practicing the skills of throwing and catching.

Teaching Games

Y **When teachers use games, the game reinforces a planned objective.** Teachers select, design, sequence, and modify games to maximize children's learning and enjoyment. For example, a game of follow-the-leader can reinforce spatial awareness and relationships, direction, speed, pathways, shadowing, and visual cueing.

N Teachers incorporate games with no obvious purpose or goal other than to keep children "busy, happy, and good." Emphasis is placed on the structure, rules, and formations of the game. Teachers use games in which children are eliminated, such as musical chairs.

Making Curricula Decisions

Y **Teachers plan a movement curriculum with a scope and sequence based on appropriate objectives and outcomes for the children's developmental levels** (NASPE National Standards 1995). The curriculum includes a balance of skills and concepts designed to enhance the motor, cognitive, emotional, and social development of every child.

N Teachers plan the movement curriculum around personal interests, preferences, and background, ignoring the continuum of motor development that focuses on outcomes and objectives that are developmentally appropriate. For example, the curriculum consists primarily of large group games that are activity based, not child centered.

Teaching Educational Gymnastics

Y **Teachers present broad skill areas such as balancing, rolling, jumping and landing, climbing, and weight transfer.** They plan numerous opportunities for exploration of these skills in a variety of situations appropriate to children's ability and confidence levels.

N Teachers expect all children to perform the same pre-determined stunts, such as forward rolls or cartwheels, regardless of their skill level, body composition, and level of confidence.

Teaching Rhythmical Experiences and Dance

Y **The movement program includes a variety of rhythmical, expressive, creative, and culturally appropriate dance experiences designed with the motor, cognitive, emotional, and social abilities of the children in mind.** Teachers encourage children to use their imaginations and move to the sound of their individual rhythms.

N The movement program excludes all rhythmical, expressive, and creative dance experiences and does not value exposing children to a variety of cultural backgrounds. Dances designed for adults (such as folk, square, or line dances) are not modified to meet the developmental abilities of the children.

Incorporating Fine and Gross Motor Activities

Y **Teachers provide learning experiences with both fine (e.g., finger-play activities) and gross (e.g., running, throwing) motor activities within the movement curricula.**

N Teachers emphasize either gross or fine motor learning experiences to the exclusion of the other.

Source: Reprinted, by permission, from the Council on Physical Education for Children (COPEC), *Appropriate Practices in Movement Programs for Young Children Ages 3–5.* (Position Statement of the National Association for Sport and Physical Education. Reston, VA: NASPE, 2000), 8, 10, 12–14, 15.

PART THREE

Challenging Children and Teachers in Movement Programs

Assessing children's progress is important in determining their levels of learning. Program goals and practices also need periodic evaluation to continue moving toward providing developmentally appropriate programs and experiences that serve all children's needs. Both aspects lead to a healthy, valuable critique essential to planning, improving, and building successful movement programs in early childhood.

6

Developmentally Appropriate Assessment

In the past, recess and free play outdoors were regarded as adequate movement experiences for preschool children. Rarely did educators assess preschool children's physical skills and knowledge.

Today, assessment of children's individual physical development and learning is essential in planning and individualizing appropriate movement experiences. The process of observing, recording, and documenting the work that children do and how they do it is a basis for educational decisions affecting children (NAEYC & NAECS/SDE 1991). This assessment can take many forms in drawing on a variety of assessment tools and measurement strategies.

Developmentally appropriate assessment helps inform early childhood practice and assists teachers in planning developmentally appropriate curriculum and learning experiences. NAEYC suggests that,

> In developmentally appropriate programs, assessment and curriculum are integrated, with teachers continually engaging in observational assessment for the purpose of improving teaching and learning.
>
> Accurate assessment of young children is difficult because their development and learning are rapid, uneven, episodic, and embedded within specific cultural and linguistic contexts. Too often, inaccurate and inappropriate assessment measures have been used to label, track, or otherwise harm young children. (1997, 21)

Developmentally appropriate assessment practices are based on guidelines that inform practice. NAEYC guidelines from *Developmentally Appropriate Practice in Early Childhood Programs* serve as criteria for the development of tools and techniques for assessing children's physical skills:

- Assessment of young children's progress and achievements is ongoing, strategic, and purposeful. The results of assessment are used to benefit children—in adapting curriculum and teaching to meet the developmental and learning needs of children, communicating with the child's family, and evaluating the program's effectiveness for the purpose of improving the program.

- The content of assessments reflects progress toward important learning and developmental goals. The program has a systematic plan for collecting and using assessment information that is integrated with curriculum planning.

- The methods of assessment are appropriate to the age and experiences of young children. Therefore, assessment of young children relies heavily on the results of observations of children's development, descriptive data, collections of representative work by children, and demonstrated performance during authentic, not contrived, activities. Input from families as well as children's evaluations of their own work are part of the overall assessment strategy.

• Assessments are tailored to a specific purpose and used only for the purpose for which they have been demonstrated to produce reliable, valid information.

• Decisions that have a major impact on children, such as enrollment or placement, are never made on the basis of a single developmental assessment or screening device but are based on multiple sources of relevant information, particularly observations by teachers and parents.

• To identify children who have special learning or developmental needs and to plan appropriate curriculum and teaching for them, developmental assessments and observations are used.

• Assessment recognizes individual variation in learners and allows for differences in styles and rates of learning. Assessment takes into consideration such factors as the child's facility in English, stage of language acquisition, and whether the child has had the time and opportunity to develop proficiency in his or her home language as well as in English.

• Assessment legitimately addresses not only what children can do independently but what they can do with assistance from other children or adults. Teachers study children as individuals as well as in relationship to groups by documenting group projects and other collaborative work. (Bredekamp & Copple 1997, 21)

A number of examples follow to show how these guidelines can be put into practice. Several types of assessment tools are included to assist teachers in selecting the assessment appropriate for preschool movement learning. Assessing children individually to determine their levels of learning is an important role performed by every teacher of young children.

Selecting appropriate assessment strategies

Assessment serves an important function in planning developmentally appropriate physical activities for young children. Motor assessment leads to knowledge about a child's skill development and to information teachers and parents can use to set goals and create learning activities that advance skill development (Folio & Fewell 2000). Accurate assessment of children's movement skills and knowledge provides the needed direction for planning appropriate success-oriented experiences that enable children to develop skills that will assist them in being physically active throughout their lives.

Assessment that is shared with parents also serves to inform and promote parent involvement in children's motor skill development. Preschool movement learning demands an approach that uses a variety of assessment methods or tools to collect information about the ever-increasing skill and knowledge of young children. A developmentally appropriate assessment plan also requires an approach allowing for collecting and storing assessment information.

Because preschool movement education programs are relatively new in early childhood settings, resources are limited that specifically discuss assessment of preschool movement and provide appropriate tools and strategies. Most available sources focus on elementary school-based physical education programs. Teachers should have little difficulty adjusting these assessment tools for use in preschool settings because most are specific to the precontrol and control levels of skill development. These assessment ideas provide examples for teachers in developing their own tools for recording preschool children's physical skill development.

The criteria for assessment in preschool movement education follow guidelines similar for assessment of other skills in the early childhood classroom. The following assessment criteria developed by the Southern Early Childhood Association (SECA/SACUS) are useful suggestions when developing assessment strategies for preschool movement education programs:

Assessment must be valid. It must provide information related to the goals and objectives of a program.

Assessment must encompass the whole child. Programs must have goals and assessment procedures that relate to children's physical, social, emotional, and mental development.

Assessment must involve repeated observations. Repeated observations help teachers find patterns of behavior and avoid quick decisions that may be based on unusual behavior by children.

Assessment must be continuous over time. Each child should be compared to his or her own individual course of development over time rather than to average behavior for a group.

Assessment must use a variety of methods. Gathering a wide variety of information from different sources permits informed and professional decisions. (SACUS 1992, xi)

What should be assessed?

In the past decade many professional education organizations first struggled to determine what works in different school subjects and clearly define *best educational practice* (Zemelman, Daniels, & Hyde 1993) and then how best to assess children's learning. These organizations developed national standards for learning in their curriculum areas. The National Association for Sport and Physical Education's "Content Standards in Physical Education" and sample assessment techniques illustrate assessment options appropriate for physical education programs (NASPE 1995).

The guidelines for physical education are based on the goal of helping children become physically educated or physically active for a lifetime. To be *physically educated,* a person has learned the skills needed to participate in a variety of physical activities, is physically fit, engages regularly in physical activity, knows the benefits of involvement in physical activities, and values the contribution of physical activity to a healthful lifestyle. Achievement of the goal of becoming physically educated is an ongoing process intended to take place over the lifetime of an individual.

In a developmentally appropriate program, different parts of the definition of being physically educated come into focus as children grow and develop. The emphasis in early childhood is on learning fundamental move-

ment skills and participating in regular physical activity and less on the fitness, knowledge, and values parts of the definition. Later, as middle school or high school students, they will emphasize fitness and knowledge as their bodies mature and they begin to participate in sport games that require knowledge of rules and strategies for play.

Content standards in physical education specify "What children should know and be able to do" (NASPE 1995, vi). The intent is to identify essential areas of knowledge and skills that should result from a quality movement education program. Not every child will achieve standards by a particular age. The guidelines simply assist in teacher planning. Because it is not developmentally appropriate to set a specific grade level or age at which children should meet particular standards, NASPE standards represent benchmarks for every two years, K–12. These serve as guidelines in planning appropriate curricular experiences.

Preschool movement portfolio

To accurately assess children's progress in a developmentally appropriate preschool movement program, a portfolio system helps teachers record and store information about each child's physical skill development. The portfolio is a purposeful, integrated collection of actual exhibits and work samples showing effort, progress, or achievement in one or more areas over a period of time (SACUS 1992; Melograno 1998). The movement portfolio presents a broad, genuine picture of children's physical development.

The type of portfolio a teacher uses depends on the needs the portfolio serves. Development of information to be placed in the movement portfolio involves the child and the teacher in compiling the materials, discussing them, and making decisions about the learning (SACUS 1992). Teachers are concerned about accurately recording a child's progress toward a mature form of individual physical skills and at the same time noting his understanding of the movement concepts related to those skills.

Most preschool children are in the exploration and discovery stages of physical development. Also most are considered at the precontrol or control level of skill proficiency (levels discussed previously in Chapter 5). For these reasons portfolio assessment tools need not be complicated. Teachers simply want to observe, record, and document the children's movement work and how they do it.

The most used assessment tools for documenting development of physical skills of preschool children are anecdotal records, rating scales, work samples, simple videotaping, photos, and checklists. Each of these tools contributes to an organized portfolio system providing teachers and parents a systematic method for collection and storage of assessment information. Such a portfolio system, although specific to physical skills learning, is also a part of an early childhood portfolio available during conferences with parents and provides them with information and a picture of their child's whole development.

National standards and benchmarks

In presenting standards, sample benchmarks, and assessment examples, NASPE (1995) first defines the standard and follows by listing key points of emphasis representative of children's progress toward achieving the standard. For each standard, a variety of techniques appropriate for assessing achievement are described. Selected assessment options accompany recommended criteria for each assessment technique. Assessment ideas are examples and are not meant to be a comprehensive listing of available assessment techniques nor the best or only assessment techniques for all situations.

The following seven content standards (NASPE 1995) include appropriate emphasis for young children, sample benchmarks, and assessment examples to help teachers.

Standard 1. **The child demonstrates competency in many movement forms and proficiency in a few movement forms.**

Emphasis for the young child

• demonstrates progress toward the mature form of selected locomotor, stability, and manipulative skills
• demonstrates mature form in walking and running

Sample benchmarks

• travels in forward and sideways directions using a variety of locomotor patterns and changes direction quickly in response to a signal
• demonstrates clear contrasts between slow and fast movement while traveling
• walks and runs using mature form
• rolls sideways without hesitation or stopping
• tosses a ball and catches it before it bounces twice
• kicks a stationary ball using a smooth continuous running step
• maintains momentary stillness while bearing weight on a variety of body parts

Assessment examples

1. Teacher observation (observational record). The child travels through general space with a steady run and, upon a designated signal, performs the next locomotor action announced by the teacher (e.g., walk, hop, gallop). Observing the child's performance, the teacher marks on the checklist the child's mastery of the various critical elements (e.g., arm swing, balance, foot placement).

Criteria for assessment:

demonstrates selected critical elements of locomotor skills

responds with correct locomotor skill as named by teacher

2. *Child's drawing sample.* Children draw straight, curved, and zigzag pathways on a sheet of paper and then identify each pattern. (A child might also use modeling clay to form the pathways.)

Criteria for assessment: correctly draws and identifies the three pathway concepts

3. *Teacher observation (observational record).* The teacher uses a checklist to assess during a manipulative learning activity the degree to which the class or individual children can identify a good "personal space," work in personal space, and move in general space without bumping into others.

Criteria for assessment:

finds personal space within general space that provides maximum room for work

stays in or returns to personal space during the learning activity

moves with an awareness of others as well as space available within general space

Locomotor Skill Checklist							
Date:	Vicky	Drake	Trevor	Shan-non	Ralph	Mary	Larry
walks	X	X	X	X	X	X	X
runs	X	X		X	X		X
hops	X			X			
gallops	X	X	X		X	X	X
skips	·	X		X			

Standard 2. The child applies movement concepts and principles to the learning and development of motor skills.

Emphasis for the young child

• identifies fundamental movement patterns (skip, strike)

• establishes a beginning movement vocabulary (e.g., personal space, high/low levels, fast/slow speeds, light/heavy force, balance, twist)

• applies appropriate concepts to performance (e.g., changing direction while running)

Sample benchmarks

• walks, runs, hops, and skips in forward and sideways directions and changes direction quickly in response to a signal

• identifies and uses a variety of relationships with objects (e.g., over/under, behind/alongside/through)

• identifies and begins to use the technique employed (leg flexion) to soften the landing in jumping

Assessment examples

1. *Teacher observation.* Children play a game of Follow the Leader in which the teacher demonstrates a locomotor movement and then observes the children to determine if each child can replicate the action demonstrated. The

Checklist for Teacher Observation of Children's Movement through General and Personal Space				
Date: ___	Finds personal space	Returns to personal space throughout the learning activity	Maintains awareness of others within the general space	Comments
Tyler	X	X	X	
Logan	X	X	X	
Matt	X			
Cindy	X	X	X	

teacher varies the movement by changing the concept applied on each repetition.

Criteria for assessment:

selects proper body parts, skills, and movement concepts

responds appropriately to a variety of cues

2. Teacher observation. The children play a game of Bear Hunt by performing the actions of a story the teacher tells. A variety of locomotor and nonlocomotor movements are used. Children practice the actions before playing the game. The teacher observes the movements of each child for appropriateness of response to the verbal cues.

Criteria for assessment:

applies movement concepts while practicing basic movements

selects proper body parts, skills, and movement concepts

responds appropriately to a variety of cues

3. Class project. Children pretend they are recreating the story of Jack and Jill rolling down the hill. They play the parts of the two characters and describe and demonstrate what Jack and Jill need to do to roll sideways down the hill. A child makes a drawing that illustrates the rolling action used by Jack and Jill.

Criteria for assessment:

identifies the critical elements of rolling

demonstrates appropriate rolling movement

Standard 3. The child exhibits a physically active lifestyle.

Emphasis for the young child

• engages in moderate to vigorous physical activity

• selects and participates in activities that require some physical exertion during unscheduled times

• identifies likes and dislikes connected with participation in physical activity

Sample benchmarks

• participates regularly in vigorous physical activity

• recognizes that physical activity is good for personal well-being

• identifies feelings that result from participation in physical activities

Assessment examples

1. Teacher observation (observational record). A variety of activities with varying degrees of physical exertion are available for the children. The teacher observes and periodically records children's choices.

Criteria for assessment:

selects activities that are vigorous in nature

participates at a level sufficient to increase breathing and sweating

participates regularly in health-enhancing physical activities

2. Children's drawings. Children participate in a class-time physical activity. At the conclusion they draw pictures indicating their feelings during and following the activity. Each child explains his or her drawing to the other classmates.

Criteria for assessment:

identifies feelings following participation in physical activity

communicates likes and dislikes connected with the activity

identifies the physical changes that occur as a result of various physical activities

3. Self-assessment. Each child responds to a teacher-made questionnaire (questions read by the teacher) by circling the smiley face most appropriate to indicate how much she or he likes a physical activity.

Criteria for assessment

identifies feelings following participation in physical activity

differentiates between activities that are more or less pleasurable

Emphasis for the young child

• sustains moderate to vigorous physical activity for short periods of time

• identifies the physiological signs of moderate physical activity (e.g., fast heart rate, heavy breathing)

Sample benchmarks

• sustains moderate to vigorous physical activity

• is aware of his or her heart beating fast during physical activity

Assessment examples

1. Teacher observation. Children engage in a series of locomotor actions (e.g., timed segments of hopping, walking, jumping, galloping, running). The teacher observes the class, noting each individual child who appears to tire easily or is unable to sustain activity.

Criteria for assessment:

stops the locomotor action before the teacher signals to do so

displays obvious signs of fatigue while continuing the locomotor action

2. Event task (observational record). Children participate for several minutes in a vigorous activity. The teacher asks them to place their hands on their chests to feel the heartbeat before the activity and immediately after the activity stops. The children participate in a class discussion, asking themselves these questions:

• What is the difference between my heartbeat before the activity and now?

• Why is my heart beating faster now?

• Are any of us sweating?

• What other activities could I do to make my heart beat faster?

Criteria for assessment:

connects the faster heartbeat with vigorous activity

associates the slower heartbeat with rest

identifies other physical activities that elicit a faster heartbeat

Activity Intensity Observation Record							
Children and dates of observation	9/15	9/19	10/14	10/23	11/10	12/3	1/14
Merideth	1	2	2	1	1	1	2
Arnold	3	3	3	2	2	3	3
Leslie	3	3	3	3	3	2	3
Jeremy	1	0	0	0	0	1	0

Observation key

3= High intensity (e.g., sustains vigorous running or rope jumping leading to heavy breathing and perspiration)

2= Medium intensity (e.g., intermittent games or activities leading to occasional increased respiration and some perspiration)

1= Low intensity (e.g., sedentary games or activities leading to no visible physical change)

0= No appreciable activity (e.g., spends the most time standing or sitting)

Standard 5. The child demonstrates responsible personal and social behavior in physical activity settings.

Children begin learning and using acceptable behaviors in physical activity settings. Safe practices as well as classroom rules and procedures are the focus. Children begin to understand the concept of cooperation through opportunities to share space and equipment with others in a group.

Emphasis for the young child

• applies classroom rules and uses procedures and safe practices, with teacher reinforcement

• shares space and equipment with others

Sample benchmarks

• knows the rules for participating in the gymnasium and on the playground

• works in a group setting without interfering with others

• responds to organizational signals

• responds to rule infractions when reminded once

• follows directions given for an all-class activity

• handles equipment safely by putting it away when not in use

• takes turns using a piece of equipment

• transfers rules of the movement "gym" to the playground

Assessment examples

1. Teacher observation (observational record). The teacher notes the names of children needing to be reminded of rules and procedures after each class period and those not responding after being reminded. The teacher gives individual attention to help the child who consistently is unresponsive after being reminded of rules.

Criteria for assessment:
follows the rules or procedures established by the teacher and the class

follows a rule or procedure after being reminded

explains questioned behavior, then performs expected behavior

2. Project (observational record). From a group of examples provided by the teacher, a child selects a picture, showing one way in which she or he can share space and equipment with others in an activity.

Criteria for assessment:

accurately identifies a mark or sign of sharing

explains why this mark or sign of sharing is important

Standard 6. The child demonstrates understanding and respect for differences among people in physical activity settings.

Young children think in terms of how the world relates to them as individuals and are just beginning to be aware of their relationships with others. They are discovering the joy of playing with friends and the way social interactions make activities more fun. Social interaction for 3- through 5-year-olds focuses mainly on family. Physical education helps expand their worlds.

Emphasis for the young child

• recognizes the joy of shared play

• interacts positively with all classmates regardless of differences such as race, gender, or disability

Sample benchmarks

• enjoys participating in activities alone and with others

• chooses playmates without regard to race, gender, disability, or other differences

Assessment examples

1. Teacher observation (observational record). Children work on tasks alone and with other children. A child willingly enters both types of situations. When a child participates with others, the group works in harmony. When disputes arise, children resolve the difficulty and continue to work together. The child demonstrates these behaviors during other unstructured times.

Criteria for assessment:

demonstrates a willingness to join an activity

participates in group activities readily, as evidenced by the length of the dormant period between the teacher's introduction of the activity and the time it begins

demonstrates cooperation with others in group tasks

2. Interview. Following a group game or partner activity, a child (individually or with a group) verbalizes the similarities and differences in participating alone versus with a group or partner.

Criteria for assessment:

recognizes that participation with a partner or group requires sharing and cooperation

recognizes that sharing with others leads to such feelings as acceptance or belonging

Standard 7. **The child understands that physical activity provides the opportunity for enjoyment, challenge, self-expression, and social interaction.**

Young children's smiles and actions give evidence of their enjoyment in participating in physical education activities. To be fun for them, movement does not have to occur in a structured game or competitive event. At this early developmental level, a child plays within a group, not necessarily as a member of the group. Young children like the challenge of experiencing new movements and learning new skills.

Emphasis for the young child

• engages in physical activities

• connects positive feelings with participation in physical activity

• tries new movement activities and skills

Sample benchmarks

• enjoys participation alone and with others

• identifies feelings that result from participation in physical activities

• looks forward to physical education/movement classes

• frequently chooses to participate in physical activities

Assessment examples

1. Teacher observation (observational record). During activity within physical education class, the teacher periodically observes and ascertains a child's level of participation and involvement.

Criteria for assessment:

demonstrates active involvement in physical activity

smiles and shows both verbal and nonverbal indicators of enjoyment

2. Group task. Children work together to create a physical activity book for the classroom. Each child draws or cuts pictures from magazines of activities that look like those in a movement class. With writing/dictation assistance from the classroom teacher, a child adds his description of the activity.

Criteria for assessment:

willingly participates in the project

identifies several activities that are enjoyable

expresses positive feelings when describing the activity

Conclusion

Assessing children individually to determine their levels of learning is an important function performed by every teacher. Evaluating program objectives to make sure programs for young children are developmentally appropriate is equally important. A checklist for evaluating movement programs appears next in Chapter 7. This checklist is intended as a resource for teachers and program directors, giving them valuable information as guidance in creating developmentally appropriate movement practices for young children.

7

Movement Goals—
Evaluation and Planning

Every teacher wonders from time to time, How am I doing? Is my teaching appropriate? Is the curriculum developmentally appropriate? Am I using the best possible assessment strategies?

Program evaluation helps teachers see where they are in terms of providing quality learning experiences for children and in what ways they can improve the quality of existing programs. The developmentally appropriate preschool movement checklist provides teachers a question format for looking at their program practices. A similar process is used to evaluate early childhood programs for accreditation (NAEYC 1998). A comparable scale aids teachers in evaluating the developmental appropriateness of elementary school-based physical education programs (Stork & Sanders 1996).

Components of movement quality

The position statement on movement programs for children ages 3 through 5 by the National Association for Sport and Physical Education (COPEC 2000) details the components of quality movement programs. Each component is accompanied by criteria describing appropriate practice. The checklist following is constructed in a comparable manner to help teachers and administrator/directors identify specific strengths and weaknesses within preschool movement programs.

The teacher or group of teachers may use the checklist as a tool in evaluating the program along with the school or center administrator/director. It calls for thoughtful reflection on and comprehensive knowledge of ongoing practices. Objectively judging the extent to which practices within the preschool movement program are developmentally appropriate suggests careful evaluation of each aspect of a component.

Summarizing program evaluations

Obtaining a summary score is not the aim of evaluation. A unique feature of the preschool movement checklist is that it does not ask participants to tally personal ratings. Standard scoring systems tend to lead to strategies that force program compliance rather than providing teachers the opportunities to move in the direction of developmentally appropriate practice and what is best for children. Such scoring systems used to compare teachers or programs often result in a form of cheating to achieve higher scores. The purposeful omission of a final tally in this book's checklist format is to encourage greater objectivity.

Teachers and administrator/directors concentrate on goals for program improvement. They keep in mind that the purpose of evaluating the preschool movement program is to encourage real, positive change toward developmentally appropriate practice within the movement education program.

Developmentally appropriate preschool movement checklist

Teaching developmentally appropriate movement to preschool children requires much thought and evaluation. The following checklist will be useful for teachers in assessing current practice and building better programs.

Curriculum

Movement curriculum needs an obvious scope and sequence based on goals and objectives that are age appropriate.

Do you ...

❑ Develop goals, objectives, and guidelines for progressive development of the content?

❑ Map out the curriculum for the year as well as make more specific daily plans?

❑ Provide a balance of experiences using different skills and concepts, not just those that interest you the teacher?

❑ Provide a variety of learning experiences that capture the interest of all children?

❑ Set up the physical education program to enhance the development of the whole child, including the cognitive, psychomotor, and affective domains?

❑ Create activities that challenge children to think, socialize, and benefit physically?

Teaching strategies

Movement exploration, guided discovery, and creative problem solving are the predominant teaching strategies employed in an effective program.

Do you ...

❑ Provide children with the opportunity to make choices and actively explore their environment?

❑ Offer children different equipment to select from and allow them to move freely from one activity to another?

❑ Avoid highly structured, lesson-type activities in which all children are expected to perform the same? For example, in an effective program children are not asked to perform the exact same movements at the same time as their peers to the same beat of music.

❑ Do you prepare a stimulating and challenging movement environment for all children (for example, providing a variety of different stations for exploring and practicing balance to allow children to select the points where they want to begin)?

❑ Give every child individual feedback?

Development of movement concepts and motor skills

Children need frequent and meaningful age-appropriate learning and practice opportunities.

Do you ...

❑ Provide practice opportunities to enable individual children to develop a functional understanding of movement concepts (i.e., body awareness, space awareness, effort)?

❑ Integrate movement concepts and motor skills into all areas of children's learning and classroom life?

❑ Encourage children to participate in a variety of activities designed to facilitate individualism and creativity (for example, children dancing to portray their interpretations of falling leaves or blooming flowers) instead of activities that require one correct answer?

Cognitive development

Movement activities are best designed with both physical and cognitive development of the child in mind.

Do you . . .

❑ Encourage children to question, integrate, analyze, communicate, and apply cognitive concepts?

❑ Use exploratory and problem-solving teaching methods?

❑ Employ activities that integrate classroom learning (for example, math, science) with movement experiences?

❑ View the movement program as contributing to other areas of the curriculum?

Affective development

Children need many opportunities to practice age-appropriate social skills.

Do you . . .

❑ Give children tasks that let them practice the skills of cooperation, taking turns, and sharing (for example, children taking turns on a balance beam or trading equipment with others)?

❑ Actively encourage the development of social skills and use conflicts as teachable moments (for example, using an argument over a ball as an opportunity to help children work out conflicts on their own)?

❑ Recognize that some children may not be ready to consistently exhibit appropriate social skills and mediate problems when appropriate?

❑ Help all children experience the satisfaction and joy of regular physical activity, both in and out of school?

Integration of movement with other curricular areas

Effective learning environments are structured to permit the interweaving of appropriate movement challenges for all children into many different curricular topics.

Do you . . .

❑ Use your movement class to integrate, whenever possible, the concepts, abilities, and actions that emerge through guided exploration and discovery (for example, using a variety of different types of balls for catching activities to reinforce learning about color and size)?

Fitness

Effective programs recognize the importance of children learning to value physical activity as a lifelong habit.

Do you . . .

❑ Help children to consider fitness a byproduct of participation in regular physical activity? For example, after an appropriate period of continuous locomotor movement, do you discuss with children what is happening to their bodies during exercise?

❑ Encourage children to participate in physical activities outside the classroom (such as during recess and at home) to learn the joy and value of exploring their physical capabilities as a lifetime pursuit?

Assessment

Systematic assessment is based on knowledge of developmental characteristics and on ongoing observations of children as they participate in physical activities.

Do you . . .

❑ Use developmental characteristics of children and observational information to individualize teaching and plan objective-oriented learning experiences?

❏ Use assessment to identify children with special needs and communicate these needs to parents?

❏ Evaluate the program's effectiveness, including both the curriculum and teaching?

❏ Assess children's skill development, but not solely on the basis of physical skills tests or standardized fitness tests?

❏ Measure children's progress by other means than the number of times they can successfully perform a physical skill in an artificial testing situation?

Active participation for every child

All children need activities that allow them to remain active but provide for appropriate short intervals of rest.

Do you . . .

❏ Avoid continuous, extended aerobic activity in your program? For example, children should not be expected to participate in adult-type aerobic dance activities in which everyone does the same thing at the same time.

❏ Recognize that children need brief rest periods when participating in particularly strenuous activities? For example, after galloping for 60 seconds children need 20–30 seconds to rest before moving again.

❏ Maximize activity time? Children should not wait to be chosen for teams, wait in lines to run a relay, stand idle due to a lack of equipment, or play sedentary games (such as Duck Duck Goose).

Dance/rhythm experiences

Effective movement programs include a variety of rhythmical and expressive dance experiences.

Do you . . .

❏ Design dance activities with the physical, cultural, emotional, and social characteristics of the children in mind?

❏ Provide a variety of rhythm experiences, not just those that may interest you the teacher?

❏ Encourage children to use their imaginations and move to the sound of their individual rhythms?

❏ Modify cultural dances, if used, to meet the developmental needs of children?

Educational gymnastics

Broad skill areas such as balancing, rolling, jumping and landing, climbing, and weight transfer are an important part of the curriculum.

Do you . . .

❏ Provide children with many different opportunities to explore gymnastic (stability) skills (for example, providing mats for rolling and requesting a climbing apparatus for the playground)?

❏ Present skills in a variety of situations appropriate to the children's ability and confidence levels?

❏ Avoid expecting all children to perform the same movements or predetermined stunts (such as requiring all children to do forward rolls or a specific sequence of gymnastic skills)?

Games

Teachers or children select games that are designed, sequenced, or modified to maximize learning and enjoyment.

Do you . . .

❑ Avoid including traditional sport games (such as softball, soccer, football, hockey) as part of the preschool movement program?

❑ Encourage children to play a role in designing game-type activities (for example, suggesting "Jenny and I made up a game; she rolls the ball to me, and I bounce it back to her")?

Gender-directed activities

Both girls and boys need equal access to all activities.

Do you . . .

❑ Encourage, support, and socialize girls and boys equally toward successful achievement in all aspects of movement activity?

❑ Avoid using gender as a factor in dividing children into groups (for example, assigning girls to the balance beam station while assigning boys to play with balls)?

Competition

Activities should emphasize "try again," effort, self-improvement, participation, and cooperation instead of winning and losing.

Do you . . .

❑ Avoid having children participate in activities that label them as winners or losers?

❑ Avoid requiring children to participate in activities that compare one child's performance against another's (for example, "Mary hit the target 10 times; you should be able to do that too ")?

Success rate

Children need the opportunity to practice skills at high rates of success adjusted for their individual skill levels.

Do you . . .

❑ Design activities in ways that allow children to practice skills independently and confidently, avoiding the pressure of having to perform at the same level of other children (for example, children practicing locomotor skills concentrate on their own movement rather than compare their skills to others)?

❑ Avoid having children participate in activities that are too easy or too hard and instead have them work at skill levels appropriate for them?

❑ Provide task extensions for children with higher levels of skill and easier variations as an option for children who are less skilled?

❑ Allow children to develop skills according to their abilities and interests (for example, knowing that, if a child desires, it is appropriate for him to spend all his time at one station, throwing, for instance, compared to walking a balance beam)?

❑ Avoid placing children in small groups or partner situations in which their success is limited, resulting in a lack of skill development? For example, in throwing and catching with a partner, more time is spent chasing the ball than practicing throwing/catching skills.

Class size

Individualized teaching is possible by assigning one adult to no more than nine or ten 4- and 5-year-old children at one time.

Do you . . .

❑ Assign younger children to even smaller groups, increasing their opportunities for exploration and guided discovery?

Frequency of movement programs and play

Physical education or movement is an integral part of the total education program.

Do you . . .

❏ Provide daily opportunities for quality movement learning, exclusive of free play?

❏ Schedule movement activity experiences on a daily basis?

❏ Plan and organize movement programs as part of the total education program and integrate them into the curriculum daily (for example, allowing 30 to 60 minutes per day, with each class exposed to a variety of skill themes and movement concepts)?

❏ Regularly schedule indoor and outdoor play experiences to enhance planned movement experiences?

Facilities

Both indoor and outdoor areas should be available, with adequate space for children to move freely and safely.

Do you . . .

❏ Avoid, as much as possible, canceling movement classes because of other uses of the facilities or because of weather?

❏ Avoid restrictions on movement activities due to lack of space and/or appropriate areas for movement (for example, knowing that narrow hallways or small classrooms are not effective places to teach movement activities)?

Equipment

Enough equipment should be available so each child benefits from maximum participation (for example, every child is provided a ball; no time is spent waiting for a turn with a ball).

Do you . . .

❏ Avoid asking children to wait in line to use a large apparatus (for example, offering several other activities instead of providing only one balance beam, so children do not wait long periods of time to have a turn)?

❏ Match equipment to children's sizes, confidence levels, and skills (for example, having balls of different sizes and that are soft and easy to grasp; racquets or bats with large striking surfaces and smaller grips and that are lightweight)?

❏ Modify or substitute equipment when appropriate (for example, using balloons for volleying instead of balls)?

❏ Provide children with junior-size equipment such as low nets and goals?

Safe environment

Children need to exercise in a physically and psychologically safe environment that allows them to explore their capabilities.

Do you . . .

❏ Provide appropriate activity space, with each child having enough space to move without bumping into another child?

❏ Provide opportunities for children to participate in self-selected activities that lead to feelings of self-confidence and self-worth?

❏ Provide a variety of activities and tasks with a range of possibilities thus creating a positive learning environment?

❏ Consider each child's readiness to learn?

Individual and free expression

Children are encouraged to use movement as a form of individual expression.

Do you . . .

❑ Provide opportunities for children to ask questions and find individual solutions to problems through movement (for example, asking children to "Find the best way to balance on three body parts without falling over")?

❑ Encourage children to express themselves freely?

❑ Avoid requiring children to move in prescribed ways or meet set standards of performance?

Fine- and gross-motor activities

Movement programs provide learning experiences with both fine-motor (such as finger play) and gross-motor (such as running, throwing, kicking) activities.

Do you . . .

❑ Ensure that fine-motor learning experiences are as available as gross-motor activities?

Repetition

Children need a variety of learning experiences throughout the year that emphasize the same motor skill so that they may develop skilled movement patterns.

Do you . . .

❑ Ensure that skills are repeated through the year and not taught just once, providing little opportunity for children to develop a foundation of motor patterns (for example, focusing on kicking, throwing, or catching in various activities at different times during the year)?

Family-teacher communication

Teachers need to work in partnership and communicate regularly with families.

Do you . . .

❑ Inform families about the movement curriculum, with the intent of promoting family involvement in children's motor skill development (for example, sharing observations of children's skills in family newsletters about the movement program)?

Using the checklist to rate progress

Individual teachers and programs may find value in creating some personally meaningful numbering scale to allow periodic review and reevaluation of progress (see "Progress Summary" as a tool). For instance, using a rating of *1* can indicate that the goal for a given component is *not* being met or perhaps that practices related to the program component occur rarely or seldom. A rating of *2* could indicate that criteria are being partially met when evaluators believe there is some evidence of goals being met. This rating suggests there is room for substantial improvement. A rating of *3* can indicate that all criteria/goals are fully met, with the desired practices related to the program component being a regular and ongoing part of the physical education experience.

The preschool movement checklist could also provide space for teachers and administrator/directors to write comments. Comments spark positive further assessment of current practices, elicit determination of whether practices are appropriate in a manner other than as described, and offer a guide to outlining goals for improvement. Comments also help teachers clarify why they engage in certain practices and how they can improve inappropriate practices. When administrator/directors work together with teachers to complete the checklist and provide comment, they gain a more comprehensive understanding of movement education as subject matter and of the teacher's goals.

Tracking program progress

After completing the preschool movement checklist and setting goals for improvement, teachers and administrator/directors may determine target dates for reevaluation. Reviewing the checklist at regular intervals helps teachers maintain awareness of appropriate practices and provides guidelines for improving practices. To monitor program quality over time, a progress summary (see chart opposite) is a useful log.

This progress summary is a comprehensive program evaluation tool. Preschool movement program assessment cannot be completed in a single day or even on the basis of several classroom observations. To assess overall program practices demands careful curriculum examination, investigation of school policies, evaluation of protocols, and scrutiny of teacher-child interactions.

Upon completing the checklist for developmentally appropriate preschool movement, the teacher may decide to engage in her own continuing education to gain understanding of the practical applications of the developmentally appropriate standards. Likewise, administrator/directors may rethink center policies and/or reallocate funds or space.

Conclusion

Assessment and evaluation are frequently forgotten parts of the early childhood movement education program. Developmentally appropriate assessment can inform practice and assist teachers in planning developmentally appropriate curriculum and learning experiences. Evaluating the program provides information on curricular, assessment, and teaching practices that may need changing or updating to provide developmentally appropriate physical activity experiences for all young children.

Progress Summary—Developmentally Appropriate Movement Program Evaluation for Preschool

Evaluations/Ratings

Movement program components	Date:	Date:	Date:	Date:	Date:	Date:
1 Curriculum						
2 Teaching strategies						
3 Concepts and motor skills						
4 Cognitive development						
5 Affective development						
6 Integration into other curricula						
7 Fitness						
8 Assessment						
9 Active participation						
10 Rhythmical experiences						
11 Educational gymnastics						
12 Games						
13 Gender-directed activities						
14 Competition						
15 Success rate						
16 Class size						
17 Frequency of program and play						
18 Facilities						
19 Equipment						
20 Safe environment						
21 Individual/free expression						
22 Fine- and gross-motor activities						
23 Repetition						
24 Family-teacher communication						

Conclusion

Making Preschool Movement an Education Priority

One principle of fitness training is called the *overload principle*. It suggests that to benefit from skill development and fitness-related activities one needs to do more of these activities today than yesterday and more tomorrow than today. Levels of fitness and skill increase the more a person practices. In creating and expanding upon developmentally appropriate movement programs for young children, this principle is appropriate.

Taking steps to ensure active, fit children

Physical activity programs for young children in early childhood settings are relatively new. Few center administrator/directors or teachers can expect to implement developmentally appropriate movement programs overnight.

Developing an effective program takes time. Space, financial and teaching considerations, and limitations at school and child care facilities can slow down the process. However, increased focus on skill development is critical to the health and physical well-being of children. The overload principle is an approach to creating and expanding movement programs and giving them the needed push for success.

Educators can use developmentally appropriate practices in movement programs for young children (COPEC 2000), as outlined in this book, to push for implementing change in their centers and schools. The push continues as teachers initiate more practices today than they did yesterday and more tomorrow than they did today.

Effective practices in movement programs for young children are a guide (see helpful tools in Appendix C) as teachers begin to create movement environments, curricula, teaching approaches, and assessment that ensure the right of every child to participate in daily physical activity.

Teacher challenges

The challenges and responsibilities of each adult who works with young children and movement education are these:

Create movement curriculum with scope and sequence based on goals and objectives that are appropriate for alll young children.

Use a range of teaching strategies that emphasize exploration, guided discovery, and creative problem solving.

Give children chances to make choices and actively explore their movement environments.

Serve as facilitators, preparing a stimulating environment and challenging activities.

Provide frequent and meaningful age-appropriate learning experiences and practice times, which enable children to develop a functional understanding of movement concepts and skill themes.

Structure the movement learning environment to include appropriate movement challenges and, whenever possible, integrate movement with other curricular areas.

Value physical activity and convey to children its importance as a lifelong habit.

Create assessment tools and strategies that are based on objectively observing and recording children's successes to individualize teaching and evaluate teacher and program effectiveness.

Create environments that encourage children to be actively involved in movement.

Encourage children to participate in a variety of rhythm and dance experiences designed to encourage using their imaginations and moving in response to their individual body rhythms.

Provide opportunities for children to develop individual skills and apply these skills in dance, gymnastics, and game-style experiences.

Support cultural and social equality in all movement experiences.

Emphasize self-improvement, participation, and cooperation.

Provide opportunities for skill practice that lead to high rates of success.

Limit class size to allow for more individualization in teaching.

Provide quality movement learning experiences daily, allowing for the gradual development of desired movement patterns.

Create environments with adequate space for children to move freely and safely both indoors and outdoors.

Create an environment fostering maximum participation, where children benefit because each child has appropriate equipment.

Plan and organize movement experiences as part of the total educational program.

Encourage children to use movement as a form of individual expression.

Emphasize the development of all motor skills throughout the school year.

Communicate regularly with families, informing them about the movement curriculum and their children's progress.

In doing these things educators empower and enable children to learn the importance of physical activity in their lives and to become physically active and healthy for a lifetime.

In providing regular vigorous physical activity, teachers give children three important gifts, which Gallahue characterizes as "the opportunity to experience the joy of efficient movement, the health benefits of physical activity, and a lifetime as confident, competent movers" (1995, 125).

Appendixes

Movement Concepts
"I Am Learning"

I am learning **what** my body does, **how** and **where** my body moves, and the ways **my body relates** to myself, other movers, and objects.

Action awareness: "I am learning **what** my body does."		
Locomotor skills	**Stability skills**	**Manipulative Skills**
walking	turning	throwing
running	twisting	catching and collecting
hopping	bending	kicking
skipping	stopping	punting
galloping	rolling	dribbling
sliding	balancing	volleying
leaping	transferring weight	striking with rackets
climbing	jumping and landing	striking with long-handled instruments
crawling	stretching	
chasing/fleeing	curling	
	swinging	
	swaying	
	dodging	

Effort awareness: "I am learning **how** my body moves."					
Time		Force			Flow
Speeds	**Rhythms**	**Degrees of force**	**Creating force**	**Absorbing force**	**Dimensions**
slow	beats	strong	starting	stopping	single movements
medium	cadence	medium	sustained	receiving	combinations of movements
fast	patterns	light	explosive	stabilizing	transitions
accelerating			gradual		

Space awareness: "I am learning **where** my body moves."			
Space	**Directions**	**Levels**	**Pathways**
self space	up/down	high	straight
shared space	forward/backward	middle	curved
	right/left	low	zigzag
	sideways		
	clockwise		
	counterclockwise		

Body awareness: "I am learning about the **relationships** my body creates."			
With myself			With other movers and objects
Body parts	**Body shapes**	**Roles**	**Locations**
head, neck, ears, eyes, nose, shoulder, knee, heel, arms, waist, chest, stomach, hips, leg, bottom, foot, spine, back, elbow, wrist, hand, fingers, ankle, toes	big/small	leading	near to/far from
	curved/straight	following	over/under
	wide/narrow	mirroring	in front/behind
	twisted	unison	on/off
	like/unlike	alternately	together/apart
		solo	facing/side-by-side
		partner	around/through
		group	

Skill Themes and Movement Concepts

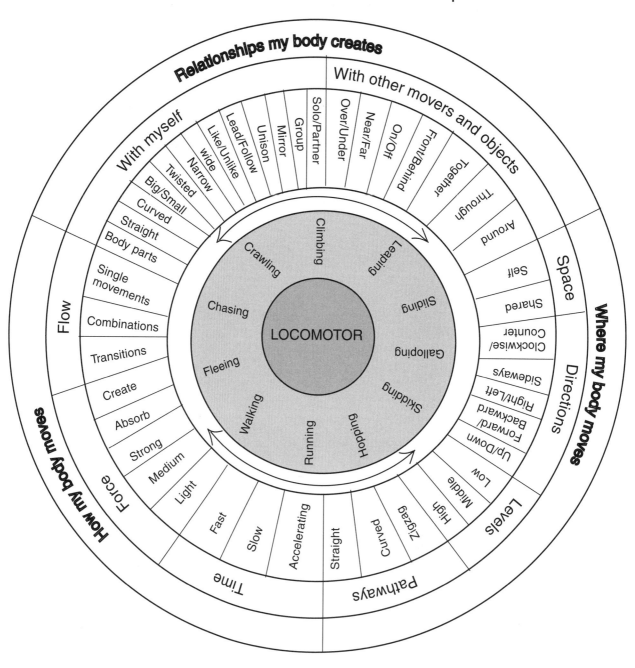

The three wheels (locomotor above, stability and manipulative on pp. 93, 94) are tools for teachers in planning appropriate movement activities for preschool children. A wheel's inner, shaded section (skill theme and encircling related skills) is stationary. The outer section (comprised of concepts and related knowledge components) rotates. By pinpointing any specific skill within a skill theme and rotating the outer section to align any movement concept, an unending variety of explorations is possible.

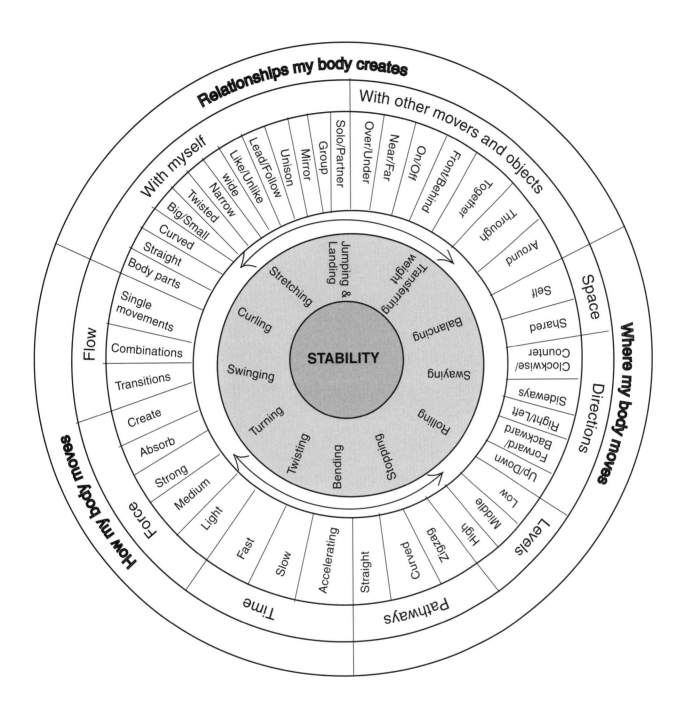

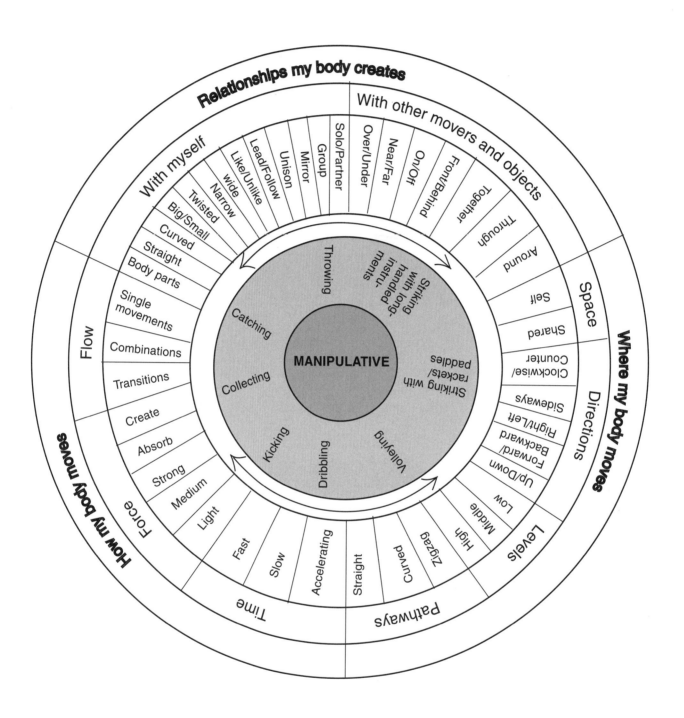

Source: Adapted, by permission of McGraw-Hill, from G. Graham, S. Holt-Hale, and M. Parker, *Children Moving: A Reflective Approach to Teaching Physical Education* (Mountain View, CA: Mayfield, 2001), 28.

Tools for Planning Preschool Physical Education Activities

Barlin, A.L. 1979. *Teaching your wings to fly: The nonspecialists guide to movement activities for young children.* Santa Monica, CA: Goodyear.

A program of dance movement activities for teachers of 3- to 12-year-olds presents a large selection of music and instruments. Specific techniques communicate how to introduce the activities and support children's natural instincts and imagination.

Block, M. 1994. *A teacher's guide to including students with disabilities in regular physical education.* Baltimore, MD: Paul H. Brookes.

Two chapters in this practical book are particularly helpful for preschool teachers: one provides ways to adapt activities for specific disabilities, the other discusses how to engage the active participation of young children with disabilities in developmentally appropriate physical education.

Gallahue, D.A. 1999. *Developmental physical education for today's children.* 4th ed. Madison, WI: Brown & Benchmark.

Written for university students in physical education, early childhood education, and elementary education, this book is designed particularly for those taking a first course in children's physical education. It gives teachers a helpful framework to approach teaching children movement activities based on a developmental perspective.

Graham, G., S.A. Holt/Hale, & M. Parker. 2001. *Children moving: A reflective approach to teaching physical education.* 5th ed. Mountain View, CA: Mayfield.

This comprehensive textbook is for teachers wanting to implement a quality elementary physical education program. It describes the skill theme approach to teaching physical education and provides information on child development, appropriate instruction, curriculum, and assessment in the movement setting.

Grant, J.M. 1995. *Shake, rattle, and learn: Classroom-tested ideas that use movement for active learning.* York, ME: Stenhouse.

Movement-based learning activities for pre-K through sixth grade are tied to nine content areas: practicing communication, experiencing stories and poetry, interpreting the environment/human relationships/societal issues, working with visual design and spatial relationships, and investigating rhythm.

Hammett, C.T. 1992. *Movement activities for early childhood.* Champaign, IL: Human Kinetics.

More than 100 pages of developmentally appropriate movement activities are included, all based on use of skill themes. Learning tasks sort into locomotor, ball handling, gymnastics, and rhythm activities. Lesson plans outline each activity's objective, vocabulary, equipment, and safety and organizational procedures for presenting the activity to children.

Pica, R. 1990. *Preschoolers moving and learning.* Champaign, IL: Human Kinetics.

This book provides written movement lessons with accompanying audiocassettes designed for use with 3- to 5-year-old children. The lessons highlight the development of locomotor skills, nonlocomotor skills, movement concepts, and the use of imagery within a rhythmical movement experience.

Pica, R. 1998. *Experiences in movement with music, activities, and theory.* Albany, NY: Delmar.

Teachers wanting to understand and use the movement curriculum in early childhood education will find information on the benefits of movement, lesson planning, creating and maintaining a positive learning environment, and bringing movement education outdoors.

Pica, R. 1999. *Moving and learning across the curriculum: 315 activities and games to make learning fun.* Albany, NY: Delmar.

This source book includes activities designed to make movement part of the early childhood curriculum by integrating it with art, language arts, mathematics, music, science, and social studies.

Sanders, S.W. 1992. *Designing preschool movement programs.* Champaign, IL: Human Kinetics.

This book is designed to help teachers develop and direct a developmentally appropriate movement program for children ages 3 through 5. It outlines the importance of movement in educating young children and tells how early exposure to structured movement activities benefits children throughout their lives. More than 100 developmentally appropriate activities are included and organized by skill themes. The book gives eight weeks of example lesson plans to start teachers toward designing and planning their own developmentally appropriate lessons.

Stinson, W.J., H.H. Mehrof, & S. Thies. 1993. *Quality daily thematic lesson plans for classroom teachers: Movement activities for pre-k and kindergarten.* Dubuque, IA: Kendall Hunt.

The authors present ideas for the development of themes in the classroom and movement setting. Collaborative themes created by the classroom teacher and a movement education specialist include such examples as "My Body" and "The Seasons."

Torbert, M., & L.B. Schneider. 1993. *Follow me too: A handbook of movement activities for three- to five-year-olds.* Reading, MA: Addison-Wesley. Available from NAEYC.

This resource offers research as a background for using movement games in early childhood settings, a perceptual motor chart indicating the skills involved in suggested activities, suggestions for parent involvement, and directions for making equipment.

Websites

www.pecentral.com

For health and physical education teachers, parents, and students—this site provides the latest information about developmentally appropriate physical education programs for children and youth. It includes a Preschool Physical Education section, plus an e-mail newsletter, equipment sources, and links to other Websites.

http://pe.central.vt.edu/adapted/adaptedsites.html

Sources and links are given for helping to adapt physical education for children with disabilities and developmental delays.

www.aahperd.org/naspe

The National Association for Sport and Physical Education promotes professional development and practice in sport and physical activity through scientific study and dissemination of research-based and experiential knowledge to educators and the public.

www.naeyc.org/resources

The National Association for the Education of Young Children focus on improving the quality of services for children from birth through age 8. All NAEYC Position Statements are online and downloadable. The *Young Children* Searchable Index contains article information and annotations of articles published since 1985. A search form helps educators locate articles of interest and need.

Suggested Starter Equipment for Movement Curriculums

What follows is not a complete list but equipment that will get your movement curriculum off to a good start. Included are short descriptions of each item—equipment you will need to do many activities in this book.

Balance beams

Balance beams give children a chance to practice balance skills by moving on a narrow strip of wood usually 4 to 6 inches wide and less than 30 inches off the ground. Balance beams are usually purchased from a physical education equipment company. These beams are expensive but are usually of high quality and durable.

Balance boards

A balance board is a fun way to help children develop balance skills by constantly placing them off balance. A balance board is a small platform raised off the ground usually with a 2-inch by 10-inch narrow base of support that children sit or stand on.

Balls

Preschool physical education programs call for a variety of lightweight foam, rubber, and plastic balls. Foam balls are easy for children to throw, catch, and kick. Rubber playground balls 8 to 10 inches in diameter provide children more challenge and can be used to practice bouncing skills when children are ready. Small plastic balls are used to throw, catch, and strike. Old tennis balls also can be hit off a tee with a bat and can be used to play catch.

Bats

Plastic bats are better than wooden bats to use when introducing striking skills. Plastic bats are lighter, safer, and easier for a young child to swing. Bats are usually about 28 inches long and 2 to 4 inches in diameter. Foam bats also are light and have the added advantage of a larger diameter head, giving children more chance for success.

Beanbags

Both square and cubed beanbags are great for throwing, catching, and balancing. Square beanbags should be 5 inches by 5 inches and filled with plastic pellets. Cubed beanbags are easier to catch because they better fit a child's hands.

Carpet squares

Small square or rectangular carpet samples have many uses, such as pretend 'lakes' to **jump** into. Usually thrown away when they are out of date, most businesses gladly donate samples to schools.

Cones

Traffic cones are used as boundary markers and as tees off which children can strike balls with paddles or bats.

Foam bowling pins

Unbreakable Ethafoam bowling pins 3 or 4 inches in diameter are great for targets and stacking. Two-liter plastic soda bottles are good alternatives.

Foam crawl-through shapes

These are made of 2-inch-thick unbreakable Ethafoam. Each 3-foot-by-2-foot crawl-through obstacle has a colored band and a small, matching geometric shape. These are used for body awareness skills and to help children identify colors and shapes. Large cardboard boxes are good alternatives; cut large holes in the boxes in desired geometric shapes.

Foam hockey sticks

Made of Ethafoam material, these foam sticks are safer than plastic hockey sticks and are excellent for teaching the hockey or golf swing. For young children, use sticks with 24-inch handles.

Foam stilts

These stilts let children experience walking 8 inches off the floor while they learn dynamic balance. These stilts are durable even for adults and have a safe Ethafoam base with plastic stick.

Hoops

Hoops usually come in 24-, 30-, and 36-inch diameters and are made from plastic. Smaller diameters are best for young children.

Jump ropes

The best type of jump rope to use with young children is one 7 feet long with plastic beads along the length to add extra weight to help children swing the rope over their heads. A longer rope tends to tangle; a shorter rope is more difficult for children to get over their heads. Bulk rope cut into 7-foot-lengths works almost as well as plastic beaded jump ropes.

Launch boards

A great way to help children catch successfully is to use a launch board. When a child steps on one end of the board, a beanbag on the opposite end flies into the air within catching distance. (Launch boards are easily made following simple instructions.)

Mats

Mats are expensive but essential if your program is going to introduce rolling skills to children. If your school does not have mats, it is better that rolling not be taught.

Paddles

These are perfect for introducing children to striking skills. The paddle face is made of light, durable Ethafoam. Three different available lengths of plastic handles give children the opportunity to practice striking using both short- and long-handled paddles.

Punchball balloons

These heavy rubber balloons are durable and move slowly through the air so children have a better opportunity to learn to throw, catch, and strike. Balloons should be inflated to a diameter of about 16 inches.

Records, tapes, and CDs

You'll find dozens of sources of music for use in a preschool movement program.

Rhythm sticks

Rhythm sticks are about 5/8 inches in diameter and a foot long and are made of wood or plastic. Children strike them together during rhythm activities.

Ribbon sticks

Children use ribbon sticks to perform expressive rhythmic movements. Sticks are 18 inches long. Ribbons range from 6 to 12 feet long. Younger children need shorter ribbons.

Scarves

Scarves can be thrown, caught, and used in rhythm activities. Lightweight, silk-like scarves fall slowly when tossed—great for catching. Scarves for young children are usually 11 to 16 inches square.

Scoops

Plastic scoops serve as extensions of children's hands and arms to help develop their catching skills. Homemade scoops can be made from plastic milk jugs.

Target board

This is a plywood target that children can throw at both overhand and underhand. Targets can be constructed of materials other than plywood. Teachers should not feel limited to using a predesigned target board.

Wedges

Foam wedges can be purchased through most physical education supply companies or made from a block of dense foam.

Source: Reprinted, by permission, from S. Sanders, *Designing Preschool Movement Programs* (Champaign, IL: Human Kinetics, 1992), 116–18.

Gross-Motor Development—Widely Held Expectations

For 3-year-olds—

• walks without watching feet; walks backward; runs at an even pace; turns and stops well

• climbs stairs with alternating feet, using handrail for balance

• jumps off low steps or objects; does not judge well in jumping over objects

• shows improved coordination; begins to move legs and arms to pump a swing or ride a trike, sometimes forgetting to watch the direction of these actions and crashing into objects

• perceives height and speed of objects (like a thrown ball) but may be overly bold or fearful, lacking a realistic sense of own ability

• stands on one foot unsteadily; balances with difficulty on the low balance beam (four-inch width) and watches feet

• plays actively (trying to keep up with older children) and then needs rest; fatigues suddenly and becomes cranky if overly tired

For 4-year-olds—

• walks heel-to-toe; skips unevenly; runs well

• stands on one foot for five seconds or more; masters the low balance beam (four-inch width) but has difficulty on the two-inch-wide beam without watching feet

• walks down steps, alternating feet; judges well in placing feet on climbing structures

• develops sufficient timing to jump rope or play games requiring quick reactions

• begins to coordinate movements to climb on a jungle gym or jump on a small trampoline

• shows greater perceptual judgment and awareness of own limitations and/or the consequences of unsafe behaviors; still needs supervision crossing a street or protecting self in certain activities

• exhibits increased endurance, with long periods of high energy (needing increased intakes of liquids and calories); sometimes becomes overexcited and less self-regulated in group activities

For 5-year-olds—

• walks backward quickly; skips and runs with agility and speed; can incorporate motor skills into a game

• walks a two-inch balance beam well; jumps over objects

• hops well; maintains an even gate in stepping

• jumps down several steps; jumps rope

• climbs well; coordinates movements for swimming or bike riding

• shows uneven perceptual judgment; acts overly confident at times but accepts limit setting and follows rules

• displays high energy levels; rarely shows fatigue; finds inactivity difficult and seeks active games and environments

Source: Reprinted, by permission, from S. Bredekamp and C. Copple, *Developmentally Appropriate Practice in Early Childhood Programs*, Rev. ed. (Washington, DC: NAEYC, 1997), 102.

Fine-Motor Development—Widely Held Expectations

For 3-year-olds —

• places large pegs into boards; strings large beads; pours liquids with some spills

• builds block towers; easily does puzzles with whole objects represented as a piece

• fatigues easily if much hand coordination is required

• draws shapes, such as the circle; begins to design objects, such as a house or figure; draws objects in some relation to each other

• holds crayons or markers with fingers instead of the fist

• undresses without assistance but needs help getting dressed; unbuttons skillfully but buttons slowly

For 4-year-olds —

• uses small pegs and board; strings small beads (and may do so in a pattern); pours sand or liquid into small containers

• builds complex block structures that extend vertically; shows limited spatial judgment and tends to knock things over

• enjoys manipulating play objects that have fine parts; likes to use scissors; practices an activity many times to gain mastery

• draws combinations of simple shapes; draws persons with at least four parts and objects that are recognizable to adults

• dresses and undresses without assistance; brushes teeth and combs hair; spills rarely with cup or spoon; laces shoes or clothing but cannot yet tie

For 5-year-olds —

• hits nails with hammer head; uses scissors and screwdrivers unassisted

• uses computer keyboard

• builds three-dimensional block structures; does 10–15-piece puzzles with ease

• likes to disassemble and reassemble objects and dress and undress dolls

• has basic grasp of right and left but mixes them up at times

• copies shapes; combines more than two geometric forms in drawing and construction

• draws persons; prints letters crudely but most are recognizable by an adult; includes a context or scene in drawings; prints first name

• zips coat; buttons well; ties shoes with adult coaching; dresses quickly

Source: Reprinted, by permission, from S. Bredekamp and C. Copple, *Developmentally Appropriate Practice in Early Childhood Programs*, Rev. ed. (Washington, DC: NAEYC, 1997), 105.

Using Recyclable Materials to Make Equipment

One-, Two-, and Three-Liter Bottle Bats

For striking movements (as in golf, floor hockey or a baseball swing, etc.) these bottle bats work well with young children because of the fat batting surface yet small handle for easy manipulation. Here's another good use for recycled plastic bottles.

Construction

1. Rinse the bottles and allow the inside to dry.

2. Using a 5/8-inch-diameter dowel rod 20 inches long, drill a starter hole on the end of the dowel.

3. Place glitter, small jingle bells or confetti inside the bottle.

4. Place the dowel inside the bottle. From the outside bottom of the bottle, put a washer around a small screw and then screw the bottle to the dowel (the washer helps keep the plastic from cracking around the screw).

5. To fill in the space around the dowel in the mouth of the bottle, use playdough. When it dries, it acts as a caulking to stabilize the bat handle and keep the contents safely inside the bottle.

6. Decorate the bottles with puff paint, permanent markers, or stickers.

Jingle Jugs

Use these jugs as targets for a variety of ball handling activities such as throwing, rolling, tossing, or kicking. Jingle jugs also serve as markers, obstacles, or traffic cones in activities. Placing items inside adds visual appeal or creates attention-catching noisemakers.

Construction

1. Rinse out bottles and allow the inside to dry.

2. Place jingle bells inside the bottles along with visually appealing content such as glitter, confetti, or ribbons.

3. For safety, glue the lids onto the bottles.

4. Decorate the outside with permanent markers, puff paint, or stickers.

5. For making heavier bottles, use sand or small-pebble gravel inside.

Plunger Tee

Use a plunger as an adjustable batting tee to provide a stationary ball for practicing baseball swings. It can also be used for other object handling activities to determine which object, by size or shape, will balance or fit the tee (where the child is asked to take one object off the tee and replace it with another object).

Construction

1. Use a small drain plunger with a 12-inch handle or saw off the handle of any wooden plunger to the length of 12 to 14 inches.

2. Cut a 6- to 10-inch length of foam pipe insulation and place it over the plunger handle. The foam insulation must fit the handle snugly enough to stay in place. The foam moves up or down the plunger handle to allow adjustments for varied child heights.

3. Place a plastic funnel in the opening at the top of the pipe insulation.

4. Adjust the pipe insulation for the top to be belly-button high on each child.

5. Place a ball or balloon in the funnel.

Six-Pack Net

Use this net in practice activities of throwing, catching, and other ball-handling skills. The net provides additional visual challenges for the child as well as spatial boundaries. It should be placed low enough so as to avoid the child having to try using undeveloped or unrefined vertical tracking skills. Six-pack nets are also a good way to recycle plastic beverage rings. This same netting can be used as plastic peg board hung on the wall, with objects attached from the plastic holes.

Construction

1. Determine the length and width of the net. Some nets can be small, others long enough to hang across a room.

2. Fasten the plastic ring sections together with yarn.

3. When the net is the desired size, weave a rope of several layers of yarn through the top holes.

4. Use the yarn-rope tails to secure each end of the net stretched between chairs, trees, or other objects.

Source: Linda Carson, University of West Virginia, Motor Development Center, Morgantown, West Virginia. Used by permission.

Movement Vocabulary and Action Cue Words

Words that describe movement are a fundamental part of a child's vocabulary. To enhance a child's movement vocabulary is to enhance her overall vocabulary. This is valuable because understanding word meaning is the first step in developing oral and written communication skills. Understanding is enhanced through movement; there is an intimate relationship between language and the body (Asher 2000).

Body parts—head, neck, shoulders, back, stomach, arms, legs, hands, feet, wrists, ankles, toes, fingers, elbows, knees

Space—high/medium/low, front/back/side, up/down, big/small, curved/straight, right/left, far/near, wide/narrow

Qualities (time and force)—slow/fast, heavy/light, sudden/smooth, strong/weak, tense/loose

Relationships—over/under, on/off, near/far, inside/outside, in front/behind/around

Actions—walk, run, jump, hop, gallop, skip, leap, roll, crawl, clap, bend, wiggle, swing, shake, turn, twist, tiptoe, freeze

Additional action cue words or phrases pertain to specific movements:

In jumping—
swing (arms)
bend (legs)
reach for the sky (extend body)
give (soft landing)

In skipping—
step and *hop*

In throwing—
side (to the target)
arm (back)
step (opposite foot)
turn (torso)
let it fly (throw hard)

When children are familiar with basic vocabulary, introduce colorful variations such as bounce, bubble, crinkle, crouch, dangle, dart, fling, float, glide, lunge, melt, ooze, plunge, quiver, rise, scamper, scatter, wobble, and zoom.

Source: Adapted, by permission, from P. Werner, S. Timms, & L. Almond, "Health Stops: Practical Ideas for Health-Related Exercise in Preschool and Primary Classrooms," *Young Children* 51/6 (1996): 51; and H. Palmer, "The Music, Movement, and Learning Connection," *Young Children* 56/5 (2001): 14.

Signing for Physical Education

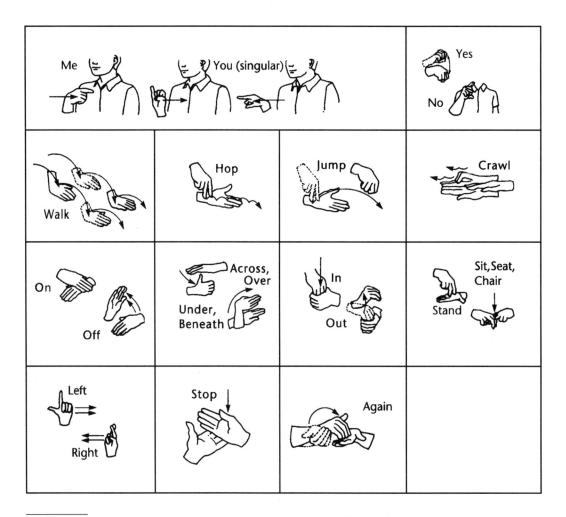

Source: Excerpted, by permission, from C.B. Eichstaedt, "Signing for Physical Education,"
Journal of Physical Education, Recreation, and Dance 49/May (1978): 20–21. Published by the American Alliance
for Health, Physical Education, Recreation and Dance, 1900 Association Drive, Reston, VA 20191.

Setting Up an Array of Movement Stations

Arranging the environment for physical activity with several movement stations, each with a range of possibilities for children's participation, allows each child to choose those activities she finds most engaging and to practice skills at the level she finds both challenging and achievable. Such an array of activity stations may also be laid out in an outdoor space.

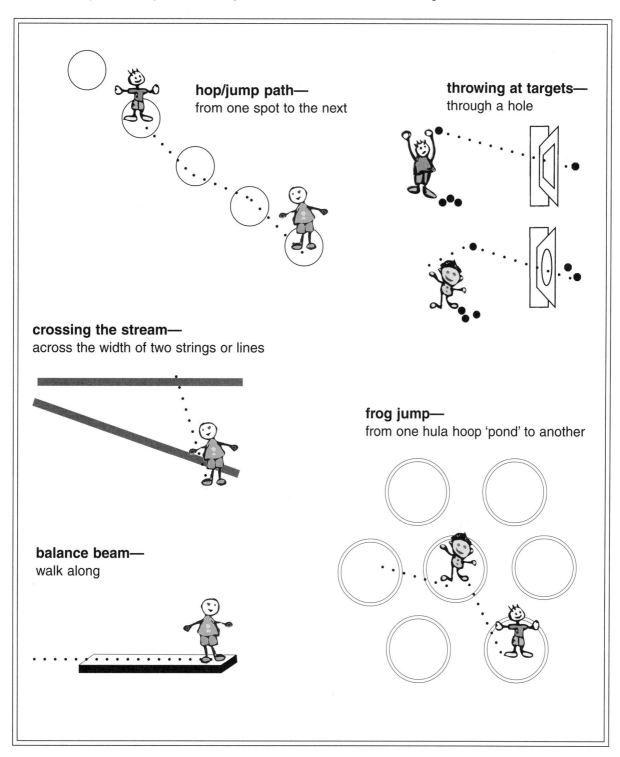

References and Resources

Allison, P., & K. Barrett. 2000. *Constructing children's physical education experiences: Understanding the content for teaching.* Boston: Allyn & Bacon.

Asher, J.J. 1996. *Learning another language through actions: The complete teacher's guidebook.* 6th ed. Los Gatos, CA: Sky Oaks.

Bar-Or, O. 2000. Juvenile obesity, physical activity, and lifestyle changes. *The Physician and Sports Medicine* 28 (11): 51–58.

Barrett, K.R., K. Williams, & J. Whitall. 1992. Developmentally appropriate physical education programs. *Physical Educator* 49 (3): 114–18.

Berk, L.E., & A. Winsler. 1995. *Scaffolding children's learning: Vygotsky and early childhood education.* Washington, DC: NAEYC.

Block, M.E. 2000. *Including students with disabilities in general physical education.* Baltimore, MD: Paul H. Brookes.

Bowman, B., S.M. Donovan, & S.M. Burns, eds. 2000. *Eager to learn: Educating our preschoolers.* Exec. summary. Washington, DC: National Academy Press.

Bredekamp, S., ed. 1987. *Developmentally appropriate practice in programs serving children birth through age eight.* Exp. ed. Washington, DC: NAEYC.

Bredekamp, S., & C. Copple, eds. 1997. *Developmentally appropriate practice in early childhood programs.* Rev. ed. Washington, DC: NAEYC.

Brophy, J., & T.L. Good. 1986. Teacher behavior and student achievement. In *Handbook of research on teaching*, 3d ed., ed. C.M. Wittrock, 328–75. New York: Macmillan.

Burk, M.C. 2002. *Station games: Fun and imaginative PE lessons.* Champaign, IL: Human Kinetics.

Buschner, C.A. 1994. *Teaching children movement concepts and skills: Becoming a master teacher.* Champaign, IL: Human Kinetics.

Campbell, L. 2001. *FUNdamental movement.* Watson, ACT: Australian Early Childhood Association.

Carson, L., & L. Griffin. 2000. Fundamental movement skills and concepts. In *Integrated physical education: A guide for the elementary classroom teacher*, ed.

L. Housner, 55–73. Morgantown, WV: Fitness Information Technology.

CDC (Centers for Disease Control and Prevention). 1996. *Physical activity and health: A report of the Surgeon General.* Atlanta, GA: Department of Health and Human Services.

CDC. 2000. *Promoting better health for young people through physical activity and sports: A report to the President from the Secretary of Health and Human services and the Secretary of Education.* Atlanta, GA: U.S. Department of Health and Human Services, CDC National Center for Chronic Disease Prevention and Health Promotion.

Chall, J.S. 2000. *The academic achievement challenge: What really works in the classroom.* New York: Guilford.

Clark, J.E., & J. Whitall. 1989. What is motor development? The lessons of history. *Quest* 41: 183–202.

COPEC (Council on Physical Education for Children). 1992. *Developmentally appropriate physical education practices for children: A position statement.* Reston, VA: National Association for Sport and Physical Education.

COPEC. 1994. *Developmentally appropriate practice in movement programs for young children ages 3–5: A position statement*, Reston, VA. National Association for Sport and Physical Education. :

COPEC. 2000. *Appropriate practices in movement programs for young children ages 3–5.* A Position statement of the National Association for Sport and Physical Education. Reston, VA: NASPE.

Cosgrove, M.S. 1992. *Inside learning centers.* ERIC, ED 356875.

Cryer, D., T. Harms, & A.R. Ray. 1996. *Active learning for fives.* Menlo Park, CA: Addison Wesley/Pearson.

Cryer, D., T. Harms, & A.R. Ray. 2000. *Active learning for fours.* Menlo Park, CA: Addison Wesley/Pearson.

Csikszentmihalyi, M., ed. 1975. *Beyond boredom and anxiety: The experience of play in work and games.* San Francisco: Jossey-Bass.

Dale, D., C. Corgin, & K. Dale. 2000. Restricting opportunities to be active during school time: Do children compensate by increasing physical activity levels after school? *Research Quarterly for Exercise and Sport* 71 (3): 240–48.

DHHS (Department of Health and Human Services). 1996. *Physical activity and health: A report of the Surgeon General.* Atlanta, GA: Centers for Disease Control and Prevention, National Center for Chronic Disease Prevention and Health Promotion.

Flynn, L.L., & J. Kieff. 2002. Including *everyone* in outdoor play. *Young Children* 57 (3): 20–26.

Folio, R., & R. Fewell. 2000. *Peabody developmental motor scales.* Austin, TX: Pro-Ed.

Gabbard, C.P. 2000. *Lifelong motor development.* 3rd ed. Boston: Allyn & Bacon.

Gallahue, D.L. 1995. Transforming physical education curriculum. In *Reaching Potentials: Transforming early childhood curriculum and assessment, vol. 2,* eds. S. Bredekamp & T. Rosegrant, 125–44. Washington, DC: NAEYC.

Gallahue, D.L., & J.C. Ozmun. 2001. *Understanding motor development: Infants, children, adolescents, adults.* 5th ed. Boston: McGraw-Hill.

Gould, P., & J. Sullivan. 1999. *The inclusive early childhood classroom: Easy ways to adapt learning centers for all children.* Beltsville, MD: Gryphon House.

Graham, G. 1992. *Teaching children physical education: Becoming a master teacher.* Champaign, IL: Human Kinetics.

Graham, G., S. Holt-Hale, & M. Parker. 2001. *Children moving: A reflective approach to teaching physical education.* 5th ed. Mountain View, CA: Mayfield.

Halsey, E., & L. Porter. 1958. *Physical education for children: A developmental program.* New York: Henry Holt.

Head Start Bureau. In press. *The Head Start leaders guide to positive child outcomes.* Washington, DC: Department of Health and Human Services, Administration for Children and Families.

Helm, J.H., & S. Boos. 1996. Increasing the physical educator's impact: Consulting, collaborating, and teacher training in early childhood programs. *Journal of Physical Education, Recreation and Dance* 67 (3): 26–32.

Javernick, E. 1988. Johnny's not jumping: Can we help obese children? *Young Children* 43 (2): 18–23.

Knudson, D. 1998. Stretching: from science to practice. *Journal of Physical Education, Recreation, and Dance* 69 (3): 38–42.

Manross, M.A. 1994. What children think, feel, and know about the overhand throw. Master's thesis, Virginia Polytechnic Institute and State University, Blacksburg.

Manross, M.A. 2000. Learning to throw in physical education class: Part 3. *Teaching Elementary Physical Education* 11 (3): 26–29.

Melograno, V. J. 1998. *Professional and student portfolios for physical education.* Champaign, IL: Human Kinetics.

Moll, L.C., ed. 1990. *Vygotsky and education: Instructional implications and applications of sociohistorical psychology.* Port Melbourne, VIC, Australia: Cambridge University Press.

Morford, L., ed. 1997. Developmentally appropriate physical education. *Teaching Elementary Physical Education* 8 (2): 3–11, 25–31.

Motor Development Task Force. 1996. *Looking at physical education from a developmental perspective: A guide to teaching.* Reston, VA: National Association for Sport and Physical Education (NASPE).

NAEYC. 1997. NAEYC position statement: Developmentally appropriate practice in early childhood programs serving young children from birth through age 8—Adopted July 1996. In *Developmentally appropriate practice in early childhood programs,* rev. ed., eds. S. Bredekamp & C. Copple, 3–30. Washington, DC: Author. Online at www.naeyc.org/resources/position_statements/daptoc.htm

NAEYC. 1998. *Guide to accreditation by the National Association for the Education of Young Children: Self-study, validation, accreditation.* 1998 ed. Washington, DC: Author.

NAEYC & NAECS/SDE (National Association of Early Childhood Specialists in State Departments of Education). 1991. Guidelines for appropriate curriculum content and assessment in programs serving children ages 3 through 8: A position statement of the National Association for the Education of Young Children. *Young Children* 46 (3): 21–38.

NASPE (National Association for Sport and Physical Education). 1992. *Outcomes of quality physical education programs.* Reston, VA: Author.

NASPE. 1995. *Moving into the future: National standards for physical education.* St. Louis, MO: Mosby.

NASPE. 2001. *Active start: Physical activity for children birth to 5 years.* Reston, VA: Author.

Payne, V., & R. Koslow. 1981. Effects of varying ball diameters on catching ability of young children. *Perceptual and Motor Skills* 53: 739–44.

Payne, G., & J.E. Rink. 1997. Physical education in the developmentally appropriate integrated curriculum. In *Integrated curriculum and developmentally appropriate practice: Birth through age eight,* eds. C.H. Hart, D.C. Burts, & R. Charlesworth, 145–70. Albany: State University of New York Press.

Perry, G., & M.S. Duru, eds. 2000. Teaching and curriculum for preschool and primary—Physical development and movement. In *Resources for developmentally appropriate practice: Recommendations from the profession,* 121–28. Washington, DC: NAEYC.

Piaget, J. [1936] 1963. *Origins of intelligence in children.* New York: Norton.

Pica, R. 1997. Beyond physical development: Why young children need to move. *Young Children* 52 (6): 4–11.

Poest, C.A., J.R. Williams, D.D. Witt, & M.E. Atwood. 1990. Challenge me to move: Large muscle development in young children. *Young Children* 45 (5): 4–10.

Rink, J. 1993. *Teaching physical education for learning.* 2d ed. St. Louis, MO: Mosby.

Rink, J.E. 1996. Effective instruction in physical education. In *Student learning in physical education,* eds. S. Silverman & K. Ennis, 171–98. Champaign, IL: Human Kinetics.

Rink, J. 2001. Investigating the assumptions of pedagogy. *Journal of Teaching in Physical Education* 20 (2): 112–28.

Rodger, L. 1996. Adding movement throughout the day. *Young Children* 51 (3): 4–6.

Rogers, C., & J. Sawyers. 1988. *Play in the lives of children.* Washington, DC: NAEYC.

SACUS (Southern Early Childhood Association). 1992. *The portfolio and its use: Developmentally appropriate assessment of young children.* Little Rock, AR: Author.

Sallis, J., T. McKenzie, B. Kolody, M. Lewis, S. Marshall, & P. Rosengard. 1999. Effects of health-related physical education on academic achievement: Project Spark. *Research Quarterly for Exercise and Sport* 70 (2): 127–34.

Sammann, P. 1998. *Active youth: Ideas for implementing CDC physical activities promotion guidelines.* Champaign, IL: Human Kinetics.

Sanders, S. 1992. *Designing preschool movement programs.* Champaign, IL: Human Kinetics.

Sanders, S. 1993. Kindergarten children's initial experiences in physical education. Ph.D. diss., Virginia Polytechnic Institute and State University, Blacksburg.

Sanders, S., & B. Yongue. 1998. Challenging movement experiences for young children. *Dimensions of Early Childhood* 26 (1): 9–18.

Siedentop, D. 1991. *Developing teaching skills in physical education.* 3d ed. Mountain View, CA: Mayfield.

Staley, L., & P.A. Portman. 2000. Red Rover, Red Rover, it's time to move over. *Young Children* 55 (1): 72.

Stanley, S. 1977. *Physical education: A movement orientation.* 2d ed. New York: McGraw-Hill.

Stoneham, L. 2001. Diabetes on a rampage. *Texas Medicine* 97 (11): 42–48.

Stork, S., & S. Engel. 1999. So, what is constructivist teaching? A rubric for teacher education. *Dimensions of Early Childhood* (Winter): 20–27.

Stork, S., & S. Sanders. 1996. Developmentally appropriate physical education: A rating scale. *Journal of Physical Education, Recreation, and Dance* 67 (6): 52–58.

Stork, S., & S. Sanders. 1999. A developmentally appropriate approach to early childhood physical activities. Paper presented at the Annual Conference of the National Association for the Education of Young Children, 10–13 November, New Orleans, Louisiana.

Sutterby, J.A., & J.L. Frost. 2002. Making playgrounds fit for children and children fit on playgrounds. *Young Children* 57 (3): 34–39.

Taylor, A., & G. Vlastos. 1975. *School zone: Learning environments for children.* New York: Van Nostrand Reinhold.

Vygotsky, L. 1962. *Thought and language.* Translated and edited by E. Hanfmann & G. Vakar. Cambridge, MA: MIT Press.

Werner, P., S. Timms, & L. Almond. 1996. Health stops: Practical ideas for health-related exercise in preschool and primary classrooms. *Young Children* 51 (6): 48–55.

Wessel, J.A., & B.V. Holland. 1992. The right stuff: Developmentally appropriate physical education for early childhood. ERIC, ED 348784.

Wickstrom, R. 1977. *Fundamental motor patterns.* Philadelphia, PA: Lea & Febiger.

Yongue, B., & K. Kelly. 1997. Developmentally appropriate use of equipment. *Teaching Elementary Physical Education* 8 (5): 13.

Zemelman, S., H. Daniels, & A. Hyde. 1993. *Best practice: New standards for teaching and learning in America's schools.* Portsmouth, NH: Heinemann.

Early years are learning years

Become a member of NAEYC, and help make them count!

Just as you help young children learn and grow, the National Association for the Education of Young Children—your professional organization—supports you in the work you love. NAEYC is the world's largest early childhood education organization, with a national network of local, state, and regional Affiliates. We are more than 100,000 members working together to bring high-quality early learning opportunities to all children from birth through age eight.

Since 1926, NAEYC has provided educational services and resources for people working with children, including:

• *Young Children*, the award-winning journal (six issues a year) for early childhood educators

• **Books, posters, brochures, and videos** to support your work with young children and families

• **The NAEYC Annual Conference**, which brings tens of thousands of people together from across the country and around the world to share their expertise and ideas on the education of young children

• **Insurance plans** for members and programs

• **A voluntary accreditation system** to help programs reach national standards for high-quality early childhood education

• **Young Children International** to promote global communication and information exchanges

• **www.naeyc.org**—a dynamic Website with up-to-date information on all of our services and resources

To join NAEYC

To find a complete list of membership benefits and options or to join NAEYC online, visit **www.naeyc.org/membership.** Or you can mail this form to us.

(Membership must be for an individual, not a center or school.)

Name _____

Address_____

City_____ State_____ ZIP_____

E-mail _____

Phone (H)_____ (W)_____

❑ New member

❑ Renewal ID # _____

Affiliate name/number _____

To determine your dues, you must visit **www.naeyc.org/membership** or call 800-424-2460, ext. 2002.

Indicate your payment option

❑ VISA   ❑ MasterCard

Card # _____

Exp. date _____

Cardholder's name _____

Signature _____

Note: By joining NAEYC you also become a member of your state and local Affiliates.

Send this form and payment to

NAEYC
PO Box 97156
Washington, DC 20090-7156